T0116500

# MaxAbility

## Who Are You? What Are You Here For?

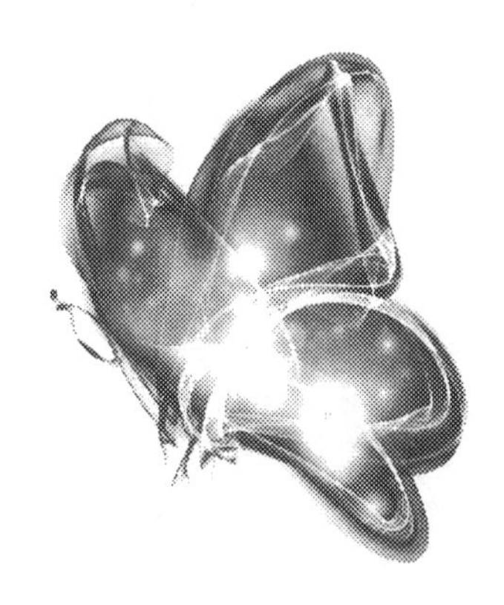

Lux Esto is the motto at K College.
Shining a light on Max, his story, everything.

# MaxAbility

## Who Are You? What Are You Here For?

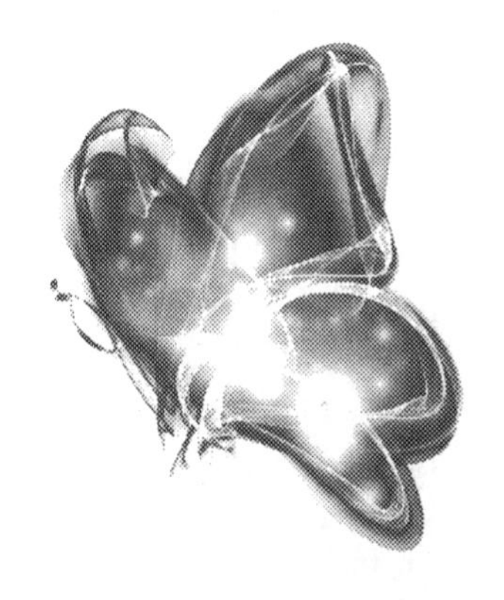

Jeanne Hess

BALBOA.PRESS
A DIVISION OF HAY HOUSE

Balboa Press books may be ordered through booksellers or by contacting:

Balboa Press
A Division of Hay House
1663 Liberty Drive
Bloomington, IN 47403
www.balboapress.com
844-682-1282



Photo Credit: Linda Nartker

Print information available on the last page.

ISBN: 979-8-7652-3705-2 (sc)
ISBN: 979-8-7652-3706-9 (e)

Balboa Press rev. date: 12/01/2022

**Dedicated to the loving memory
of Stephanie Marie Nartker**

# Table of Contents

# Foreword

### Written by Robert M. Weir

When I met Max Nartker for the first time, it was the summer of 2014. We were at the Fifth Third Ballpark, home of the White Caps minor league baseball team, in Grand Rapids, Michigan. It was the perfect place for our arranged meeting.

His parents, Ron and Linda, were there too. They all knew that I was helping Jeanne Hess write a book that, we thought at that time, would be pretty much exclusively Max's story.

Max, then a teenager, greeted me with the same pivotal questions that he had directed toward Jeanne some months before: "Who are you? What are you here for?"

But, of course, we all knew the answer. So his greeting was more jest than grim.

As we watched the game, sitting on a blanket, from the berm beyond the left field homerun fence, Max impressed me with his knowledge of sports. All sports. He truly was—and is—a walking encyclopedia of information, news, and statistics about collegiate and professional teams in various sports. Not just baseball.

He spoke this knowledge not only to me but to others around us: the families on nearby blankets, others farther away, people in the concourse as we walked to and from a concession stand.

In the following winter, on two occasions, Max and his parents, Ron and Linda, came to my home. We interviewed. Max talked in-depth about his birth, his early youth in Russia, his upbringing in Michigan, his accomplishments in school, his goals in life. He was, in some ways, advanced and intelligent beyond his years. In other ways, he was still very much a youth with hopes and dreams and aspirations. And challenges … just like the rest of us.

I easily understood why Jeanne was taken with him. This young man has something to offer to the world. And the world has something to offer to him. Just as it is with all of us.

Max has a certain power, a way of being and acting, a joy that goes beyond the physical world.

His family has a way of loving and showing love that is astounding. They, together, are a story.

I can't say that theirs is a rare story. Definitely not. For there are others out in the world who have that innate or circumstantial ability to demonstrate love far above the norm. Therefore, I can't say "just like *all* of us" when speaking about the Nartkers. But they are special. They are a positive model of what the rest of us might do if faced with the same or similar circumstances.

What are those circumstances? The opportunity to bring children from the other side of the planet into our homes and give them a chance to evoke—for the benefit of all of us—an example of our max-ability to demonstrate amazing love.

Jeanne Hess saw this wonderful characteristic in the Nartker family. In Max, she saw beauty within his gruffness, charm within his sometimes strident voice, desire and conviction that hurdles conventional social barriers. She saw his max ability.

She saw magnificence within his family.

She has the wisdom and desire within herself to write this story.

For them and her, the rest of us can be eternally grateful. The story within *MaxAbility* is a prime lesson for all of us. It is a motivation for each of us to identify, seek an understanding of, and reach fulfillment of our inner purpose. Whatever that might be.

# Preface

I'll begin with this. I believe in miracles.

Not the woo-woo kind of miracle we feel when we miraculously find a parking spot (although those miracles do exist). But rather, the life-shaping, moment-by-moment realizations that we—all people—are all connected, that we are one, healed, and wholly joined.

This book is the result of my experience with that awareness of the common thread that runs within and throughout our connective lives. *A Course in Miracles* says, "You will not rest until you know your function and fulfill it, for only in this can your will and your Father's be wholly joined." Succumbing to the great universal truths, the questions hurled at me from the lips of my friend Max Nartker were to forever change my life: "Who are you? What are you here for?" he said. With those words, the seed of a story was planted in the soil of my soul, ready to unfold.

That soil had been tilled by previous experiences that had seared themselves into my consciousness. Most notably, my Catholic-Christian-Episcopal background. I had an aunt, my dad's sister, who had entered religious life in a convent in Detroit four years before my birth. As a young child, when my family would visit the convent, I was simply overwhelmed by the majesty of the place. The high-ceiling entryway, the gentle sounds softly sluicing through the long grandiose corridors, the mystery, and the palpable faith of Aunt Gerry, wearing her aquamarine habit, that resonated with me as she visited us in the common room, the only part of the building, in addition to the chapel, where we were allowed to visit.

Years later, when I was older and she was out in the world, my aunt and I began to converse about theology, religion, and politics. I saw her then as a game-changer. I shared her radical ideas about the Church. I readily agreed with her that women belonged within and throughout the ministry of Christ, not just in subservient roles.

She was unflappable in her support of women in positions of leadership in the Catholic Church. So much so that, even on her deathbed in 2011, she implored me to continue her work. Well, you simply don't say no to an 84-year-old nun who is dying of brain cancer, so I tucked her request into a mound of soil and labeled it "future crops." After all, maybe she meant her work for the poor, underserved, and for justice within the city of Detroit.

Years before that, on March 30, 2004, another, even larger seed found its way into the recesses of my consciousness. At that time, I had maintained a 10-year-long daily meditation practice to begin my day. I was alone, seated as usual in the living room of our home in Kalamazoo, Michigan. Now, if what I am about to reveal makes you close this book and cast it aside as woo-woo fiction, then please at least give it to your most crazy friend.

Please also know that sharing this thought with you is also opening a floodgate of emotion and courage within me. For I have not said anything about this to anyone but my spiritual advisor and closest counselors who are, by law, required to keep their client's conversations confidential.

With my eyes closed in meditation, I heard a voice at the other end of my couch say, "He made himself abundantly clear."

Now I don't know about you, but I do know that when one hears a voice, one will normally turn and look to see who is speaking, wanting to know where that voice is coming from, especially in a quiet, empty house. I did. I saw no one. But I do know that the voice was real. So real that I wanted to hear more. To know more. Hoping to bring the voice back, I asked aloud, "Who is 'he'?" No answer. Only silence. It didn't take but a moment for me to realize that, obviously, I was supposed to know who "he" was. And I did know or at least had an inkling—on some level.

I journaled this event, so I remember the date. It was in 2004. Since then, I've been waiting for another voice, for further clarification. Nada. *Except* that I've been living—and sort of but not really satisfied—with my deep, deep knowing from my Catholic-Episcopalian-Christian faith journey, that "He" was Jesus. The Christ. The One.

But what mystified me more then and continues to mystify me now is: About what had he made himself abundantly clear? That's what I really want to know!

And what about that word "abundantly"? What the heck? In 2004, "abundantly" was not a common part of my vocabulary, let alone something I would use to describe the intention of "He." What I have come to know since then is what is made very clear—abundantly clear—in *A Course in Miracles,* mentioned above: *Jesus came to unite us.* The Christian Scriptures proclaim, "I and the Father are One, and You are One with Us." Metaphorically, it says "I am the vine and you are the branches." Jesus came not only to show us *His* divinity, but to enable us to reveal and experience *Ours!*

That said—and if you're still reading—so many miracles have come forth to let me know that that voice from 2004 was spot-on. He did make Himself abundantly clear. He has, since then in various ways, clearly told me what I am to do.

And it's taken me what seems like a long, long time to weave this story together. So I am also becoming clear that God wants me to practice patience and acceptance. After all, I've been busy with a career and family and coaching the wonderful young women who have chosen to play volleyball at Kalamazoo College.

As I write this now, I am grateful. Grateful for all the seeds that have been given to me. Grateful that I carefully held on to them. Grateful that, at some level of consciousness, I have been nurturing them and am able to bring them to fruition now.

This story of Max, his family, and his journey of faith is blended with the joys of love and acceptance. Their story is also blended with my story and the story of my family, my faith, and my journey through a career in education and sport.

For me, up until now or up until recent years, I have been mostly satisfied with my purpose as a teacher and coach, spiritual counselor and advisor. But, as I move into my encore career as a Kalamazoo City Commissioner, I am convinced that there simply has to be a greater purpose for me here in this life. In this moment. This is abundantly clear.

Max had it right when he asked me those questions: Who are you? What are you here for? As you will discover in this book, Max's intention at the time he spoke those words was very much on the Earth plane. He was questioning my presence in a space he had defined as his. But I also link his profound query with the statement by the voice I heard in 2004. The voice of the One who knows. I believe that His intention was to make it abundantly clear to me that I was to listen—and heed—the call from God coming through the voice of the young Max Nartker.

That is why the story within *MaxAbility* makes sense to me. Or maybe I should say, why it makes sense to me to trust that God knows where and how and with whom—you, I hope—this story will unfold tomorrow, and the rest of your tomorrows.

This is why I believe, if nothing else, this book can be—or is—an inspiration. An awakening. Therefore, I implore you to keep reading, to keep connecting the dots, and to find your own purpose through these certainly complex times.

# Acknowledgments

Brother David Steindl-Rast mused that "The root of joy is gratefulness." Given that joy is my greatest hope for this world, it goes without saying that my gratitude is oozing out of every pore, in every vessel, and with every beat of my heart. I am so very blessed in this life to have lived in a time of such great human transformation and to have had experiences that have introduced me to beautiful people who have shared this "max-able" journey.

Max, oh Max, where would we be without you? Thank you for showing up on that fateful day and for always saying "yes." Yes to Courtney's matriculation at Kalamazoo College; yes to Hornet Volleyball; yes to enthusiasm; yes to being our game announcer; yes to sharing your story, and yes to practicing patience throughout the process. As you know, the process and the product isn't what either of us envisioned, but here we are, perfectly nestled into the outcome of this moment!

Dear Nartker Family, thank you. Thank you for your daughter Courtney, who taught me about a greater love through volleyball. Ron and Linda, as parents, your conscious-shaping of your beautiful family has created such amazing opportunities for each of them. Thank you for also saying "yes" to the process of crafting this story and for contributing so much to the story itself as you journeyed alongside Max, helping him find himself as he grew into adulthood. Without you, Max wouldn't even be here. Eric, Courtney, Elena, Max, Ron and Linda, you are a blessing and a great joy to me and to all you meet. You have certainly lived your faith and planted seeds in everyone you met. Thank you from the bottom of my heart.

My story cannot be told without acknowledgement of my husband, Jim. His love, counsel, and willingness to support my career in teaching and coaching has been inspirational, to be sure. We've been each other's teachers, we've learned each other's lessons, we've been parents and now grandparents, in this wild world. I'm so grateful for you in my life, and so glad I said "yes."

Finally, without the commitment and literary genius of my editor and co-author Robert Weir, this book would remain only in spirit. After helping me with *Sportuality: Finding Joy in the Games,* Robert has spent more time helping me birth this book. His actions are many, including interviewing Max and his family, working independently on the manuscript, conversing with me about everything from the message to the language to the layout of the book, and, the most difficult of all, holding me accountable. Robert and I met originally in 2006 while both working as local volunteer advocates for a National Department of Peace, so our shared values resonate within and throughout this book. That he was able to do this work while also serving as a volunteer to help pass Michigan's anti-gerrymandering proposal in November of 2018 is admirable. My gratitude overflows. Thank you, Robert! May your great adventures continue!

# THE POWER OF STORY

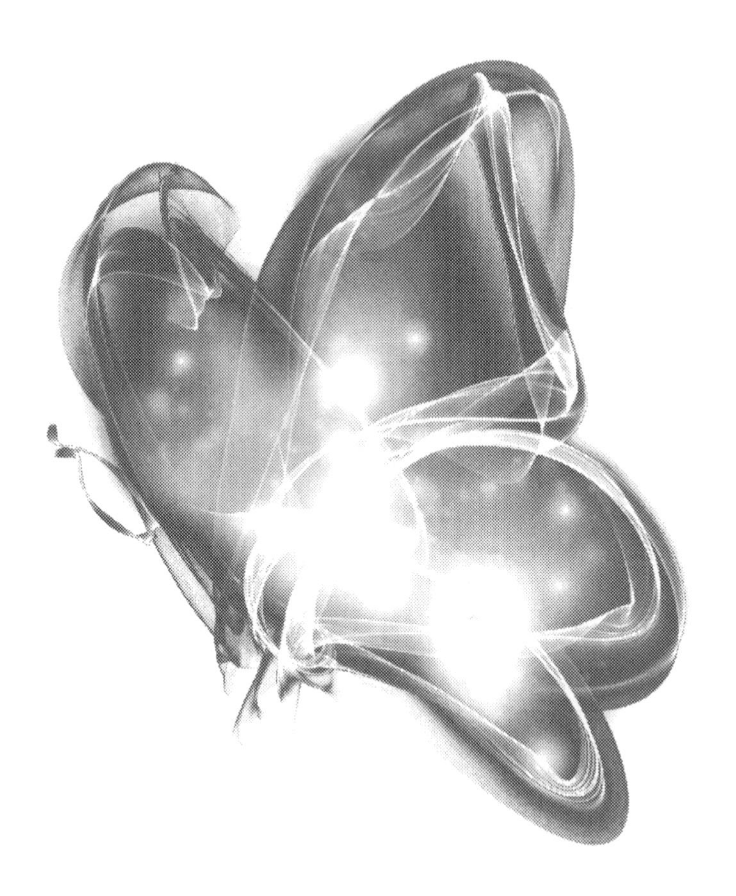

# THE POWER OF STORY

The Bible. The Sutras. The Vedas. The Quran and Hadith. The Torah, Tanach, Mishnah, Talmud, and Midrash. How often they are quoted!

Why? Because they contain some deep and significant natural or spiritual truth. They answer the "big questions" and offer guidance regarding why human beings exist on this planet: Who are we and what are we here for … both individually and as a whole?

Some sacred books offer divergent points of view regarding specific rites, rituals, and practices. But they also cover fundamental points, such as "love one another," "be kind to your sister and brother," "share and be at peace with each other."

Over time and repetition by priests, teachers, artists, storytellers, and moviemakers, the sacred stories become an innate part of human life. They form a creation template, a method of archetypical thinking that becomes a paradigm or a norm for how people, societies, and parts of societies think and act in the world.

But stories—even the old, faithful, tried-and-true stories—evolve. People change. They try new ways. New patterns of being emerge. Of course, the status quo doesn't like change. But the evolution continues anyway as people uncover new skills in the art of love and acceptance.

The people represented in *MaxAbility* are like three circles in a Venn diagram: Max is in one circle. The Nartkers and I in another. And you, the reader, in yet another. The overlapping intersections contain "The Big Questions." These are, in themselves, a universal truth because they compel us to find, discern, and define how we will employ our individual beliefs into the collective consciousness of society's whole. So, let's, together, take a look into who we are and what we're doing here. Let's examine our MaxAbilities.

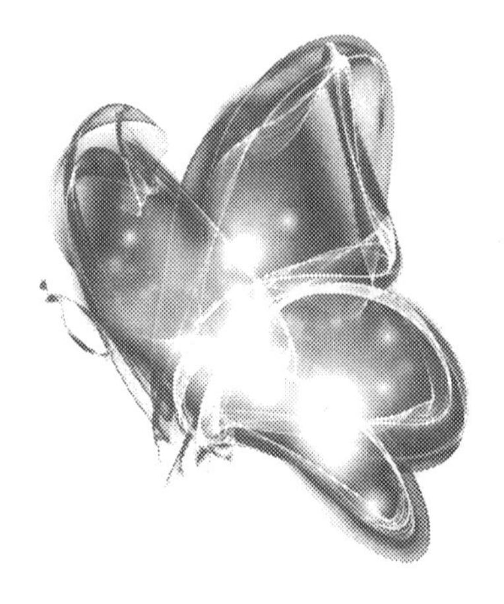

**Do something that will make a difference.**

## CHAPTER 1

# Touched by the Vertical

*"In the beginning was the Word."*

**—John 1:1**

So, have you decided what you are going to do for Lent? What do you hope to accomplish? Do you think you will be able to do it, that you will succeed? If so, then throw away that plan and come up with something that seems impossible!

Pick something that will make a difference. Something that will give you reason to turn to God and pray, "I can't do this alone. I need your help!" If your efforts don't go as planned, that's okay. Just keep coming back to God. Ask for help several times a day. Even every hour. Then, after Lent, you'll really have something to celebrate.

Why? Because the period of Lent is a time of being cleansed and seeing the light, a period of transformation that leads us to the celebration of new life—new beginning—at Easter."

As I sat in church on that Ash Wednesday, the words of my pastor, Fr. Ken Schmidt, bounded through my consciousness and resonated through my soul. "Seeing the light..." "Transformation that leads to new

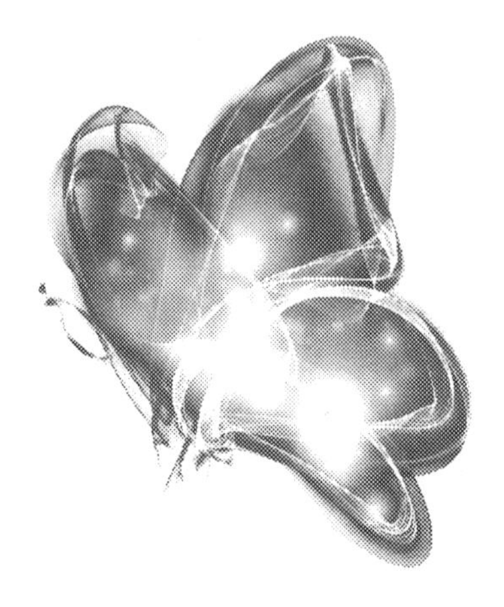

**What you believe has much to do with how you tell your story.**

life." "What do you hope to accomplish?" "If it's not going to produce change, why bother?" "Is it too easy? Do something that will make a difference." Pick something that seems impossible, a goal that compels you to pray.

Max! I couldn't help but think about Max, with his blunt, territorial dictum: "Who are you? What are you here for?"

And here was Fr. Ken, in his gentle yet assertive Catholic/Christian way, saying the same thing, challenging me to self-evaluate my person and my purpose: "What are you going to do for Lent? What do you hope to accomplish? If you don't come up with something that's hard, throw that idea away and come up with something that seems impossible."

Something that will make a difference! Like answering those timeless questions and knowing—really knowing—who I am and what I am here for.

Just as I began to project answers, Fr. Ken knocked his message out of the park one more time. "Here's your homework for Lent," he said. "How do you frame your life in a way that gives it meaning? How does your life give meaning to you? Think about your answers and maybe even write your story."

He's talking to me! The words screamed in my head. I sat up straighter. Tears welled up in my eyes. And, as anyone who knows me will tell you, that's when I feel something is really meaningful. My mental notes attempted to organize themselves.

He's talking to me! Just as Max had done when he figuratively reached into my heart in that noisy high school gymnasium ten years ago. Just as I had been talking to myself, trying to harvest enough courage to begin another monumental task and to do something (write!) that I felt was too hard, too impossible, to do. I had already written one book, and it took a lot of time, energy, and resources. Did I really have to do this again?

Then Fr. Ken finished with the extra point, the "and 1" that brought my mind racing back from that gym where Max had confronted me to the reflective quiet of St. Thomas More's sanctuary.

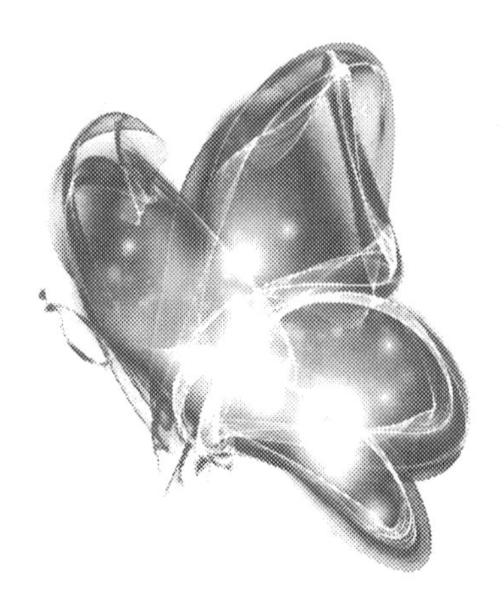

**Do something that seems impossible.**
**Do something that will make a difference.**

"See," he said, "I believe that what you believe has much to do with how you tell your story. What do you *really believe* in your mind and proclaim with your lips? What do you *really believe* in your heart and put forth with your hands? What you *really believe* will determine how—and if—you will tell your story. And when you do tell your story, does God have a place in it?"

Who are you? What are you here for?

Then Fr. Ken walked away from the pulpit and back to his chair in the sanctuary. Was he even aware that he had rolled the stone away from the tomb where I had attempted to bury the little buzz that had been nagging at me: "Tell Max's story. Write Max's story. Live Max's story."

With goose bumps coating my skin and a sob choking in my throat, I looked at the sky through the window-walls that faced me, and then my gaze focused on the hand-crafted wooden crucifix above Fr. Ken's chair. I saw a smaller crucifix atop the altar. No matter the shape or size of the symbols, the iconic figure of Jesus Christ inhabited them.

I felt my muscles shudder as though my arms wanted to involuntarily lift and extend both upward and outward, to emulate that sagging, yet outreaching figure of Christ. I felt connection with the Divine and with all humanity, which is the ultimate symbolism of the crucifixion: the vertical post reaching upward to God, the horizontal bar reaching outward to our brothers and sisters, and the power of both centered in the intersection behind Christ's head ... the center of the Christ-Mind, the center of right-thinking.

My realization on that Ash Wednesday, the day of ecclesiastical darkness when Christians accept a symbolic ashen cross on their foreheads, was that Christ had descended through the vertical plane to inwardly touch and inspire Fr. Ken, and that this priest of God had delivered his message outward on the horizontal plane directly into my consciousness.

That simple message. Work on Max's story. Write it. Write it with the energy of both the Divine vertical and the human horizontal.

Yes, I could tell myself that I've been waiting ten years since meeting Max to hear this message, delivered through Fr. Ken. But, in truth, the

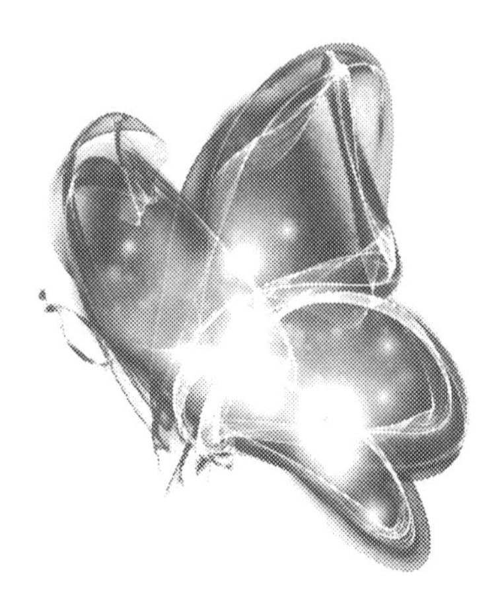

**... the knowing of another's story builds bridges and increases our connections across so many divides, whether they be physical, mental, emotional, or spiritual.**

message had been resonating in my own consciousness all that time. And I had been putting it off, setting it aside, even shunning it on too many days.

That's why I sat in my seat, hearing Fr. Ken's homily, feeling my heart swell. I muttered under my breath, "He's talking to me. Fr. Ken is talking to me. God is talking to me. Max is talking to me. Max's story is talking to me." Max's story ... the story that has been incubating in me for so long!

Do something that seems impossible. Do something that will make a difference.

"Tell Max's story. Write Max's story. Live Max's story!"

And, in doing so, write my own story—and implore you to write *YOURS*. But isn't our own story the hardest part? At my core, I am a connector, and it is from that core that I was inspired to connect the horizontal and the vertical, the birth and death, and the joy and pain of human life. You can do this too.

Sister Joan Chittester has said that it is impossible to hate another when you know their story. Not that anyone here is hating on anyone else, but the knowing of another's story builds bridges, and increases our connections across so many divides, be they physical, mental, emotional, or spiritual.

My shoulders sagged with resignation as I thought, "How to begin?" Then the obvious answer marched in. "Through resolution. With Lenten resolve." I would begin to write.

Now! During Lent, this 40-day period of preparation for Easter, the greatest feast in the Christian lectionary, the Resurrection, the coming forth and rising again.

Easter ... the epitome of the vertical plane. It's now been a few more Lenten seasons and Easters since my first attempt to write Max's story found its way to my computer screen. Now, it's time. The time has come to publish—that is, to make public—this most compelling story about a young man who's easy to meet, and so very hard to forget! Get ready to meet Max.

**Thus began a relationship that would alter our lives forever.**

## CHAPTER 2

# Shoved on the Horizontal

*"Unforgettable. That's what you are."*

**— Irving Gordon, sung by Nat King Cole**

"Max Nartker, easy to meet, hard to forget!" Max blurted with an unusually loud laugh as we sat near each other in the high bleachers. I thought he might punctuate his over-friendly comment by punching me in the arm, like a couple of buddies who had known each other for ages.

And yet it was but a few minutes ago when he had confronted me with his threatening, yet essential soul questions: "Who are you? What are you here for?"

Lest you misunderstand, Max's query was not solicitous. He wasn't like a receptionist in a professional office, asking name and nature of my business; nor like a clerk in a store, asking politely how she might offer assistance; nor like a collegiate professor or counselor, asking a student what she wants out of her academic career. Max quite bluntly wanted to know why I had invaded his territory, and there wasn't anything God-like or saintly in his tone or body language.

I responded from an equally horizontal, ego-based Earth plane with my name, rank, and serial number: "I'm Jeanne Hess, volleyball coach at Kalamazoo College. I'm recruiting players for my team. And I've come here to watch your school's volleyball team."

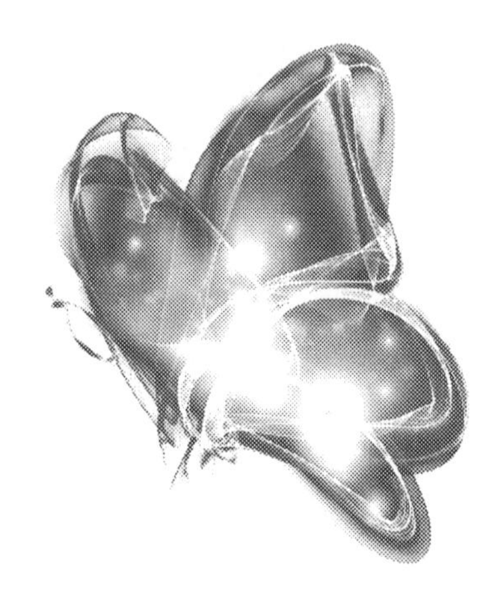

**Who are you?**
**What are you here for?**

Thus began a relationship that would alter our lives forever.

The gym at Midland High School in Midland, Michigan, was like any other high school facility where I had met so many significant people in my life, from my husband, Jim, to my teammates back in my youth, to the countless players who I've come to love through forty years as a high school and collegiate coach. This gym had a typical yellow wooden floor, emblazoned with the school mascot, the Chemic Atom, at midcourt. The wooden bleachers extended several rows upward, enough to seat an enrollment of 1500, qualifying it as a Class A school.

The gymnasium's size made it a great venue to host a wild Friday night high school basketball game, attended by the entire city. But this Saturday daytime volleyball game drew only enough people to loosely fill only a few lower rows on the lower half on the home team's side plus a smattering of folks on the visitor's side.

Sure, I could have sat anywhere. But the ample space way up on the bleachers at the very top row and toward the end of the court is my favorite place. From there, I gain a bird's-eye view of the action and am better able to take in the big picture of my recruit's world.

Usually, I sit near the rafters by myself. But on this day, there was this bespectacled, somewhat slender—let's say skinny—middle-school boy with short, brown hair who was already seated up there by himself. He eyed me warily as I approached. Then, seated and just as I was pulling my clipboard from my briefcase and getting comfortable, he turned and blasted me with his thematic questions: "Who are you? What are you here for?" It was as though he knew who was supposed to be up there in that gymnasium … and who wasn't. Apparently, I wasn't.

When I explained my purpose, he nearly shouted, "Who are you here to recruit?"

"I'm watching number 5," I said, trying to remain polite while keeping my eye on the court.

The volume of his exclamation nearly knocked me off my seat, "That's my sister!" Immediately, he added, "I don't want her going to

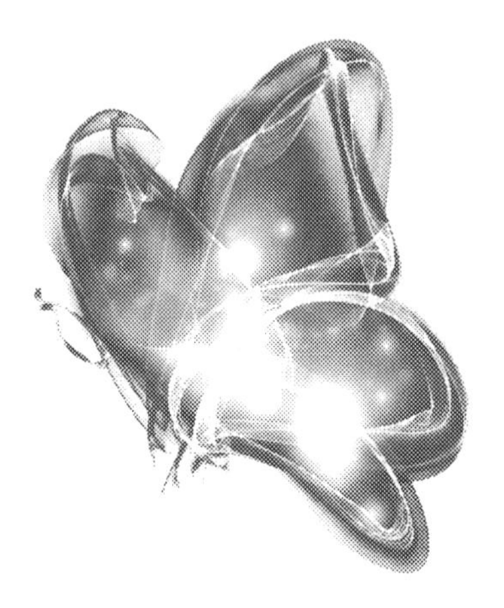

**Everything happens for a reason.**

Kalamazoo. That's three hours away, and I *don't* like things that sting!" That last one made me laugh, because our mascot is a Hornet.

Later, while driving home, I would reflect with surprise that Max knew so much about Kalamazoo College. But, during our relationship, I would learn that he is simply a fountain of information and statistics, especially in regard to sports. "He has a mind like a steel trap" goes the relative expression. Max's mind was definitely working overtime ... all the time.

Over the years, I've gotten to know Max quite well. We've become friends. As I have with his family: parents Linda and Ron Nartker; their biological children, Courtney and Eric; adopted daughter, Elena; and Max, who is also adopted. Courtney (player #5) chose to come and play at K College and was a great asset to our team, from 2008 to 2012, and who continues to inspire me with her life choices.

Max eventually became a fan of the Hornets and, with aspirations of becoming a professional play-by-play announcer, took the microphone during some of our home games to try his hand at that skill.

Each time I conversed or corresponded with the Nartkers, I reminded myself to write Max's story. Yet, it's taken me nearly a decade to put the words together.

Perhaps I delayed because the story is so complex. Or perhaps because it's so very simple, just like the questions.

Perhaps I needed to have all the experiences first. Or perhaps that was just the excuse I afforded to myself.

As I delayed, I would simply believe, as many do, "Everything happens for a reason." And then, "I must be delaying for a reason." We all do that, don't we? And then we allow that notion to linger on the surface of reality—aka procrastination—and don't take it further. You are reading my attempt at "the further."

Since the publication of my first book, *Sportuality: Finding Joy in the Games,* in which I invite readers to rethink and reframe the concepts and terminology commonly used in sport—terms like *competition, victory,* and *enthusiasm*—I have encountered so many sportual experiences that have led me to outstanding athletes, coaches, parents, and fans. Experiences

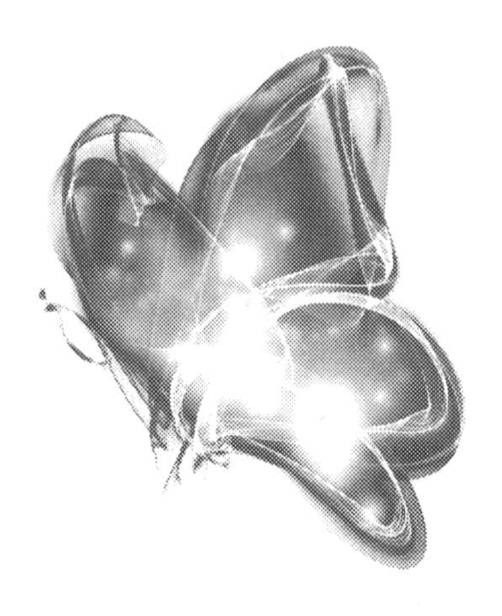

**Their story embraces the principle of inclusion, of every child being wanted and accepted for whom they are, whether by loving parents, or by a coach, or by the rest of a team.**

that led me to the greater story—the sportual story—that *is* Max Nartker. I now have had the experiences—enough experiences—that finally compelled me to tell his story.

Max's story—and the story of the entire Nartker family—is an application of the principles found in *Sportuality*. Thus, their story, while unique, is universal.

Their story encompasses the sportual words: *communication* ("to make common" and all-encompassing); *spirit* ("to breathe" and feel the purpose of life inside of you); *community* ("to have charge of together" and to become one again); and *humor, education, religion, holiness, sanctuary,* and *sacrifice.*

Their story embodies the characteristics of courageous, selfless parenting. As I have come to know the Nartker family over the years, I have seen them profess through words and actions their interpretation of sportuality. They are among my great inspirations.

Their story embraces the principle of inclusion, of every child being wanted and accepted for whom they are, whether by loving parents, or by a coach, or by the rest of a team.

Thus, this book—*MaxAbility: Who Are You and What Are You Here For?*—is a sportual book. This book indicates how to live the principles found in *Sportuality* in order to create a better life for ourselves and those we love ... even if those we love, like Max and Elena, were born to other parents in a different country half way around the world.

This book is about freedom and containment, about giving and receiving, about yin and yang. It's about choosing love over fear and living *your dream* despite what others might believe or say. It's about, as Socrates encouraged us so long ago, to "Know Thyself." And that, he said, is the beginning of wisdom.

Sport provides the perfect stage to play out these great truths. Max Nartker is the perfect spirit to advance these truths on this horizontal plane we call life. As he will often remind you, "I'm easy to meet, hard to forget."

So stay with me on this journey. By the end, you will know Max. More importantly, you will know yourself better. How? Because you will

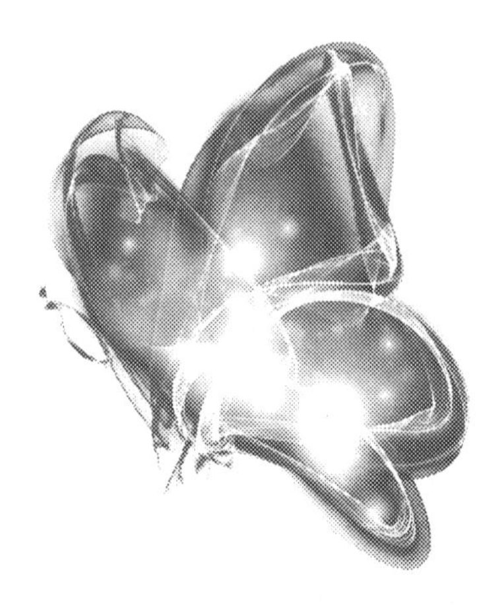

**Thank them for bringing their universal joy and love to you.**

ask and, in an increasingly conscious manner, answer those provocative, ever-present, eternal questions: "Who am I? What am I here for?"

Let Max speak to you. He speaks to me every day. As words go, "max" is pretty ubiquitous—as in "take it to the max" or "maximum load." When Fr. Ken spoke on Ash Wednesday, I was reminded that I can do more to reach my "max" ability.

Where is the "max" in your life?

Who are *you*? What are *you* here for?

Because meaning and purpose grow with reflection, time-outs like the one below will appear throughout the book. *Sportuality: Finding Joy in the Games* uses time-outs to encourage the reader to reflect on each of the 12 words in that book. Here, the point of time-outs is to encourage you to find your max ability—your gifts—your source of gratitude and joy. These can simply be mental notes, a journal, or they can even become your own story! So … TIME OUT! The coach has something to say:

**TIME OUT**

Before we begin our journey with Max, take time to recall the moment when you unexpectedly met someone new who, since then, has become a significant presence in your life. Can you remember that initial encounter like it happened yesterday? Do you still breathe in the experience? Does it still seem like a miracle, like a Divine connection, crafted right before your eyes?

Close your eyes and go back in your memory to that time, that moment. Who is that person? Where were you then? What were the circumstances of your meeting? Was it planned or did it occur by chance?

Is the person still in your life or have they moved on? Either way, look that person in the eyes and thank them for coming into your life and bringing their universal joy and love to you.

# THE POWER OF LIFE

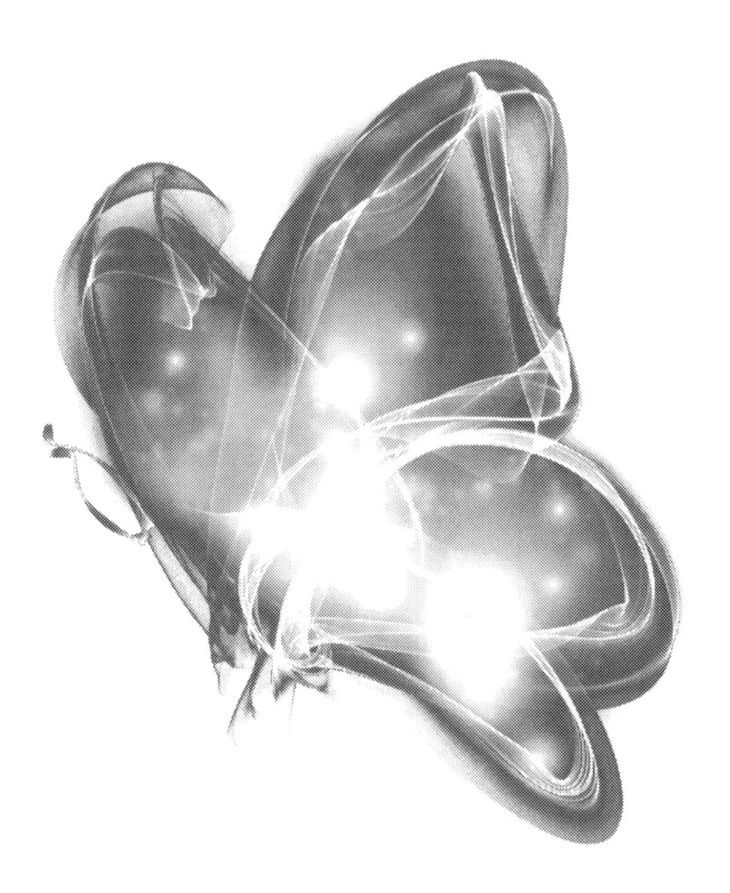

# THE POWER OF LIFE

Life will always find a way, just like a dandelion or quack grass springing through a crack in a driveway. As I began to know the Nartker family through their stories, I was inspired by Ron and Linda's strength as they clung to their desire to grow their young family, to bring new life into their home. I marveled at their ability to persevere, to face and overcome obstacles. It was then when I realized the great truth that I often reminded myself in both the parenting and recruiting processes: the apple doesn't fall far from the tree; life, lived in love and desire, will always find a way.

Because stories need to be told, I asked Linda to tell, in her own words, her stories of birth and death, of desire and adoption. While Max is the principal character in this book, without the grace of Linda and Ron who agreed to share their pain and joy, their loss and resilience, *MaxAbility* would not exist.

Max's story begins with his sister Stephanie. She is the plot trigger point, the catalyst from which the other stories in this book follow. She is the thread that continues to weave its way through the joys and complexities of life.

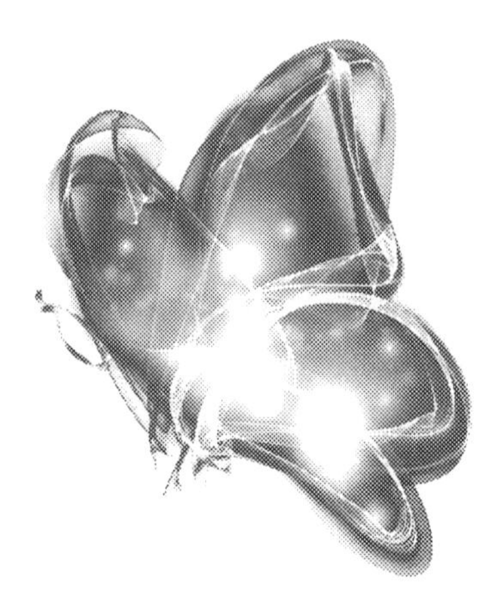

**Life was calling.**

# CHAPTER 3

# Stephanie

*"Whom the gods love dies young."*

**— Herodotus, Greek historian**

Enter Linda and Ron Nartker. The year is 1995. They have two healthy, wonderful children: Courtney, the future volleyball player, was 5, and her younger brother, Eric, was 3. But Linda and Ron felt the call to have a third child. "Should we?" they asked. "Your age …," Ron pointed out tentatively. "Yes, 35. Yes, there are risks associated with a birth at my age." "You'll be a year older by the time you give birth." "But …" "But?" "But I want to try." Life was calling.

Linda's tone was resolute. Yet, being beyond the traditional child-bearing years, she asked her doctor about amniocentesis, a prenatal test used to determine birth defects in a fetus. "You're healthy, and there's no family history of the disorder. So, no, I don't think that test is necessary," the doctor assured her.

Within a few months, Linda missed her next period and began what she called "an easy pregnancy." Anticipating a girl, she and Ron chose the name Stephanie Marie … but with some hesitation and respect for Linda's brother, who had lost a daughter, named Stephanie, 13 years earlier. "He's totally for it. Happy to have another Stephanie in the family," Linda reported to Ron.

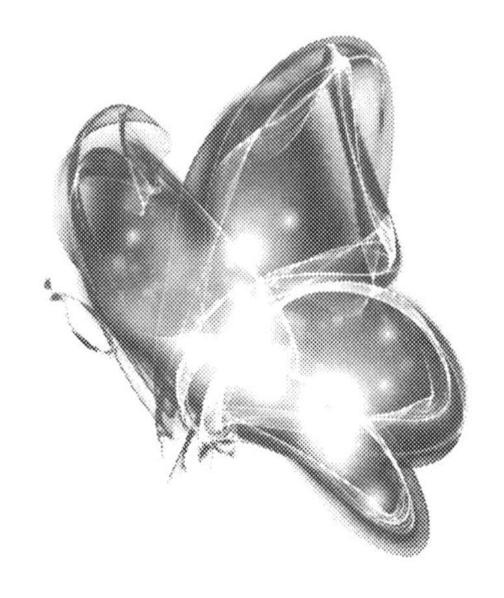

**Is this really *normal?***
**What *is* normal?**

Then came the latter weeks of her third trimester. Of this time, she relates:

> The time came for my 35-week checkup. I remember this so clearly, as if it were yesterday. It was our anniversary. Thursday, August 29, 1996. I took Courtney and Eric with me to the appointment. The doctor asked if I was sure on the due date because the baby seemed a little small. He ordered an ultrasound, which, in 1996 was still not a common part of a pregnancy. I was more excited to see whether it was a boy or a girl than to entertain the thought of anything being wrong.
>
> It *was* a girl! She had 10 fingers and 10 toes! Life is good! I did not pay any attention to how long the procedure was or the repeated measurements they were taking.
>
> Later that night, I received a call from my doctor. He asked if he could come to our home to talk with us. Soon, he was seated at our kitchen table, where so many meaningful conversations had unfolded. But, of course, I knew before he arrived that something was amiss. Even in a small town like Midland in the mid-1990s, a personal visit from a physician was rare.
>
> He said that our baby's head was too large, which indicated excess fluid on her brain, and her heart appeared to have only one ventricle. Optimistically, it could mean *just* heart surgery and a stent on her brain with the *possibility* of a *normal* life. Or, she might not survive.
>
> I felt ripped apart. The intellectual part of me understood his words as the characteristic of life and death. Things like this happen. But the emotional part within me was screaming, "Aaarrrrrggggghhhh! Not to me! Not to us? And what's this "*possibility* of a *normal* life"? Is this really *normal*? What *is* normal?"

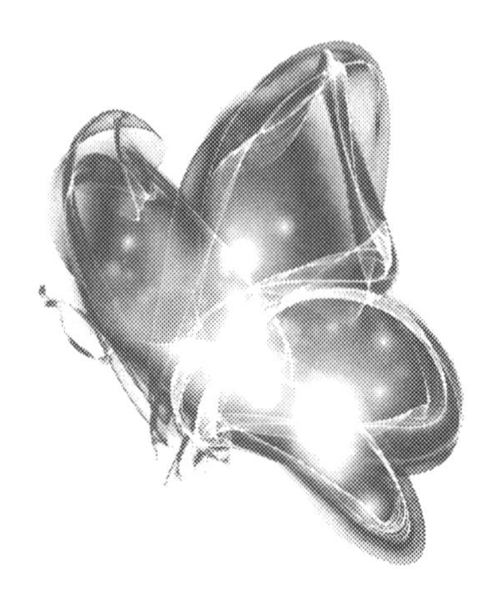

**All I wanted to do was cry.**
**But I couldn't. I had a child to**
**deliver ... healthy or not!**
**That was my only priority.**

Ron and I had an appointment the next morning, the Friday of Labor Day weekend, with a neonatal specialist. A friend volunteered to stay with Courtney and Eric. We drove to the hospital, my hands resting on my swollen belly and Ron's shaking slightly on the steering wheel. I knew the car was moving down the road, but it felt as if we were not really going anywhere. And the silence between us was deafening. Was this to become our *new normal?*

We arrived at the hospital. There, a better ultrasound machine revealed that there were two ventricles in her heart. Thank God! But, clearly, there were other structural defects. We were advised that an amniocentesis would give answers that would help us be prepared for her birth. We agreed. It would be ten or more days before we would have the results. Going into that long holiday weekend and not knowing any more than that was absolute torture.

On the following Tuesday, we had further tests with a pediatric cardiologist. He was more hopeful and provided information that would help us determine which hospital was best equipped to handle our daughter's birth and first days and weeks of her life: Covenant Hospital in Saginaw, which was closer to our home, only 30 minutes away; or Mott Children's Hospital in Ann Arbor, which was a major medical facility that could handle all of Stephanie's needs but was nearly two hours away. We absorbed that information and made no decision. We hoped that maybe, just maybe, her heart wasn't so bad. Maybe she wouldn't need surgery quite so soon after her birth.

The next few days in early September were a blur as we waited, tried to work, and selectively shared the news with family and close friends.

The following Saturday morning, I awoke with what, at first, seemed like my usual trip to the bathroom. But something

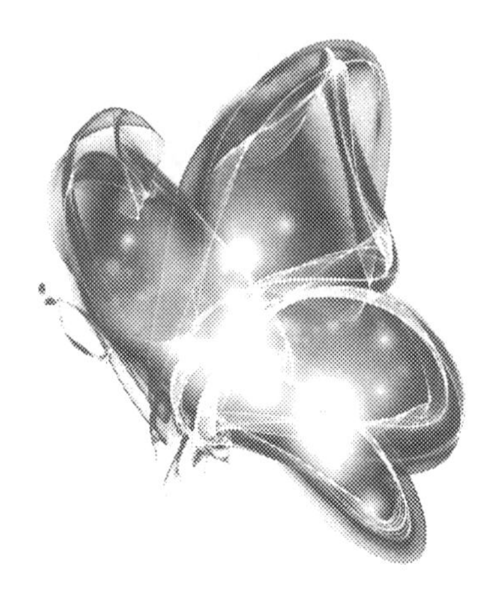

**We were optimistic. . . .**
**I knew in my heart**
**that her situation was dire.**

was not usual. My water had broken. Three weeks early! Now what?

In emergency mode, we headed to MidMichigan Medical Center, the closest hospital, with a towel between my legs. There, I was given medication to stop labor and taken by ambulance to Mott Children's Hospital in Ann Arbor. It was a long, bumpy ride.

Once there, my labor was allowed to resume but stopped again because Stephanie's heart was in distress. She would need to be delivered by Cesarean section to be born alive. And we still did not have the results of the amniocentesis. What if she were born with chromosomal abnormalities? All I wanted to do was cry. But I couldn't. I had a child to deliver ... healthy or not! That was my only priority. My years as a collegiate athlete at Michigan State University had given me the ability to stay focused during a difficult physical challenge.

Stephanie Marie was born on Saturday, September 7, 1996. She weighed 3 pounds, 10 ounces. As soon as she was out of the womb, the delivery nurses gave us a quick glimpse of our baby's tiny, frail body, and then whisked her away. She looked better than I had expected. But ... But? How could I tell? The glimpse was so short. And they would not even let me touch her! She had been in my womb for 36 weeks, then she was gone. I felt deflated. All I could do is lie there and wonder. Then I cried.

The next few days ran together with short trips to see her in the ICU as I recovered from surgery, pumped breast milk, dealt with an endless array of tests, and tried to deal with a steady stream of doctors, nurses, interns and students, each with their own specialty.

Stephanie was on oxygen but holding her own, they said. We were optimistic. Then she wasn't tolerating the breast milk, and the nursing staff was sustaining her with a sugar solution, delivered intravenously.

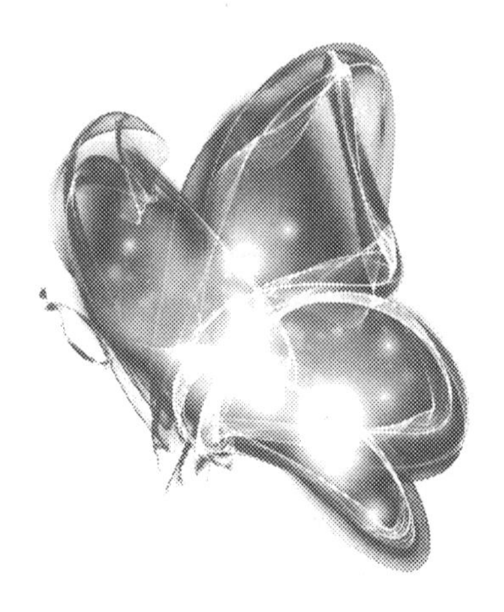

**She was comforted by being held, and so we held her, day and night.**

I was discharged on Tuesday, September 10. Stephanie had been alive three days.

Our plan was that I would go home, spend the night with Courtney and Eric, and pack a bag for a long stay at the hospital in Ann Arbor. Before we left, we visited the ICU once more. This time, we saw three white coats surrounding our tiny Stephanie, assessing her vision and hearing. We left feeling very uneasy. I knew in my heart that her situation was dire. I knew in my heart that the bag I was going home to pack wouldn't be needed.

I returned to Ann Arbor the next morning with my sister and a friend while Ron took care of personal and professional business at home. We were immediately met by one of the head doctors and escorted to a private room. The results of the amniocentesis tests were in. "Stephanie has Trisomy 18, a chromosome disorder," the doctor said. Her tone was professional, attempting to be matter-of-fact, yet the hint of emotion in her voice caused me to choke on my tears.

"In addition to the low birth weight and heart defect, there had been some physical indications. Low-set ears and clenched fists with index fingers crossed over her middle fingers," she said. "What does this mean?" I asked. She looked at me before answering. I held my breath, reminding myself that I almost always like direct answers. But this one was crushing. "It's fatal."

Now letting my tears flow freely, I called Ron. He arrived quickly, as quickly as was possible from two hours away. We never talked about the thoughts running through his mind while he drove. But I ran through a litany of questions that nearly overwhelmed me while waiting for him.

The biggest was, "How long will she live?" The answers spoken by the professionals were undeterminable: "Days, weeks, months."

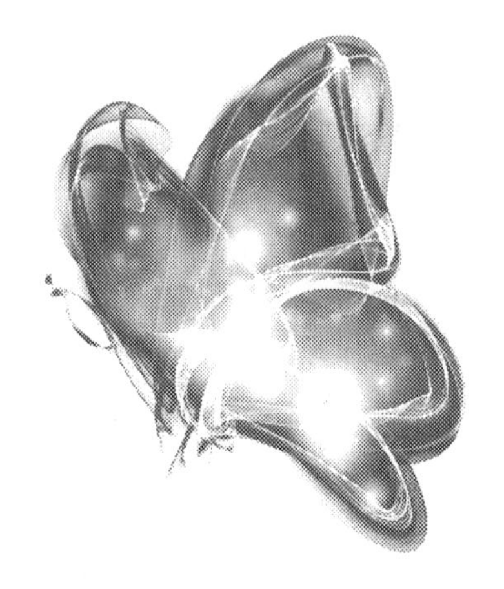

***This is so very hard.***
***I can't do this.***

The hospital personnel were caring but didn't understand me or my family. When they said, "You can leave her here and we will take care of her until she dies," I nearly screamed. *Are you kidding me?* No, that would *not* happen!

We had Stephanie baptized in the hospital and then transported to MidMichigan Medical back in Midland. She rode alone in the ambulance while Ron and I followed in our car. Another long silent drive for all three of us.

Our pediatrician was waiting for us in her room when we arrived. Stephanie was a small wrapped bundle in a large child's bed. She looked so tiny and helpless. The furniture was rearranged to accommodate our family members, and the pediatric floor became our home for the next few weeks.

Stephanie was blind and deaf, not responding to light or sound. But she was comforted by being held, and so we held her, day and night. Her frail body needed warmth. Someone stayed with her every night. My sister took a turn. Our daycare provider took a turn.

The days passed in a blur. Friends and family visited. Ron and I bought burial plots in the cemetery. Courtney and Eric went to school during the day and spent the evenings at the hospital.

Should we have a visitation or just a private burial? *This is so very hard. I can't do this.*

I would go to sleep at night, ready to let her go, but be so happy to see her in the morning.

After much discernment, I reluctantly agreed to a visitation, and was later happy to have that first awkward meeting with everyone all at once … and get it over with.

All of these logistical decisions wore me down. I needed to sleep through the night. My friend Anna took a turn of staying

**Look how desperately she's clinging to life.**

with her in the hospital. Our phone rang at 12:30 am. "Stephanie no longer has any viable IV sites in her hands or feet," Anna said.

We had a choice: to insert a central line catheter in her neck or chest to administer the sugar solution . . . or to let her go. *How do we possibly decide this?* She would be uncomfortable and on pain meds with a catheter. We agonized but knew we had to let her go.

We also now knew that we had to bring her home. Ron had wanted to bring her home sooner, but I struggled with the thought of her dying at home. We arranged for hospice care, and she came home very early Friday morning, September 27. Stephanie had been alive 20 days.

*How long would she be with us?* The doctor estimated she would live three or four days before succumbing to the effects of dehydration. *Is that all?* He was right. Our sweet Stephanie shriveled up before our eyes.

The hospital provided small bottles of sterile sugar water solution to help keep Stephanie's lips moistened. I remember how excited little three-year-old Eric was when he proclaimed, "Look, Mom! She learned how to drink herself."

My take was much different. Look how desperately she's clinging to life.

The weekend passed and Stephanie was still with us on Monday morning. After lunch, my mom was holding Stephanie, who was all bundled up in her blanket, when the hospice nurse stopped by. I remember the look on her face after she placed the stethoscope on Stephanie's chest. She was struggling to maintain a professional persona, but her heart was reaching out to me through her moistening eyes. Stephanie had passed away. September 30, 1996, 1:30 pm.

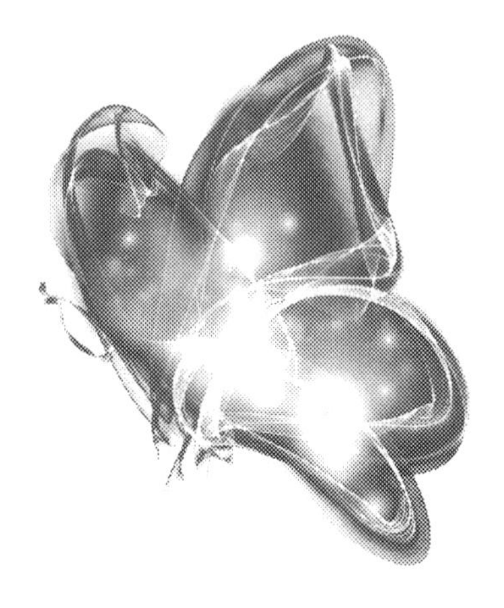

**He's here because he loves us.**

I thought I was prepared for the inevitable, but the wave of grief was overwhelming. I wanted to just keep holding her, touching her cheek with mine.

All along, Stephanie had worn a small cap and had been bundled up in a blanket so the only exposed part of her body was her face. Now, I felt her become very cold, very quickly.

The hearse showed up to take her away. They waited for us to finally let her go. Passing her body over to them, knowing I would never see her alive again, was the hardest thing I had ever done in my life.

We had one visitation session at the funeral home. A steady stream of family, friends, neighbors, and co-workers came. I had always hated, dreaded, and avoided funeral homes, but I realized that night that they serve a purpose. A very valuable purpose … for the living. "What are you here for?"

Then came the kicker. John, a co-worker who was dying of brain cancer and confined to a wheel chair, showed up. Cynically, a flash thought came to me: *Maybe he wants a preview for himself?* And I almost yelled at myself, "No. No. He's here because he loves us." Looking at him and the love he exuded for our family, I asked myself, "How could I ever excuse myself from a visitation again?"

We had one more chance to say goodbye to our baby after the visitation ended. I would never have thought that holding a rigid, cold, dead body could have meant so much.

Stephanie Marie was buried in a private ceremony the next day, October 4, 1996. I vividly remember the sight and sound of the first shovel of dirt cascading onto the tiny white casket. The thudding sound. The dirty soil staining the casket's purity. The finality. My daughter would never be seen again.

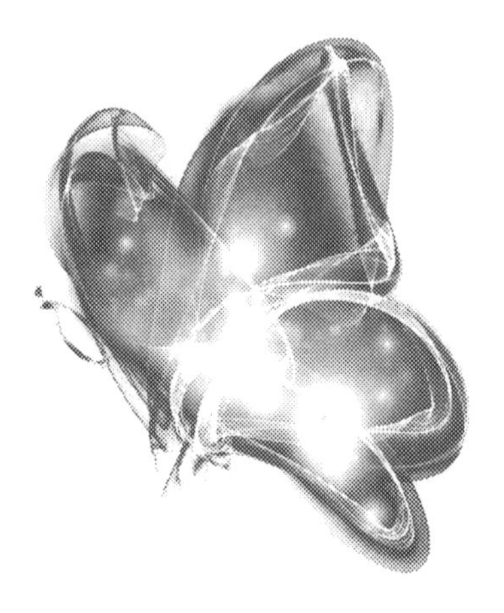

**How do we move forward from this grief?**

Linda concludes her story with that inexplicable mixture of grief blended with the inevitable knowing that she and her family must move on. "What do we do the day after we bury our child?" she asked. This was followed by the undeniable thought that her son, Eric, would turn four in three days. "I don't want to celebrate his birthday," she told Ron. "How do we move forward from this grief for our daughter?" Yet, she knew the answer. "We celebrate the life of our son. We must."

**TIME OUT**

Can you relate to Linda? What has been a similarly significant defining moment in your life, a moment when you knew you couldn't avoid an impending "bad outcome," a moment that, even if you were Shakespeare, you would never script for yourself or your world?

Bring to mind any visitations, funerals, or final good-byes you've experienced. Try to resurrect the love that you felt for that person and hold them in your heart.

If you are so inclined, take a moment to visit https://www.trisomy18.org/ to learn of the condition that defined Stephanie's life.

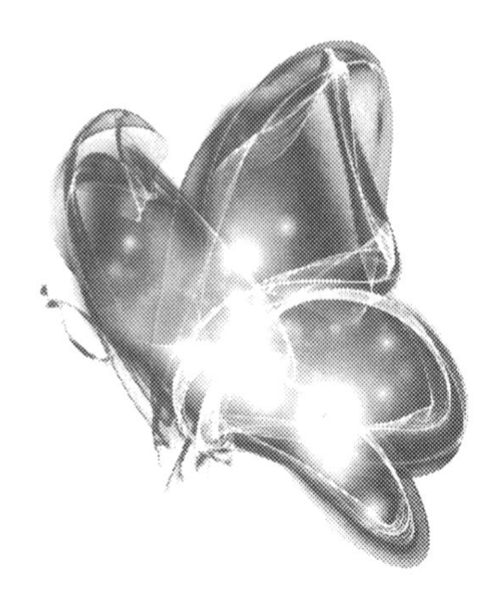

**Can *we* dare ask
what good might come from death?**

## CHAPTER 4

# Where's the Good in This?

*"There is nothing either good or bad, but thinking makes it so."*

**— William Shakespeare**

"Everything happens for a reason," people say, repeating that damnable perennial theme. Even death? Yes, of course, even death. Even death of a 23-day-old infant? "Well …," they hem and haw. "Well …"

We can look upon Stephanie's death and Linda and Ron's grief from a pessimistic perspective. We can say, "Oh, that's too bad that she died so young." Yes, we can do that. But if we truly, genuinely believe that everything happens for a reason—even if that reason doesn't seem obvious or even possible at the time—then we must also ask, "What is the purpose of Stephanie's life … and death at such a young age? What did she bring to the world?"

In search of an answer, I go back to Fr. Ken and the image of him sitting beneath the crucifix with its wooden crossbars, the ultimate symbol of that metaphysical intersection of the Divine vertical and the human horizontal.

Did Christ's disciples entertain the notion that the crucifixion would…could...lead to a resurrection? From a human perspective, that was likely far beyond their consciousness, even though Christ had told them that he would rise again from the tomb. So, if those holy men and

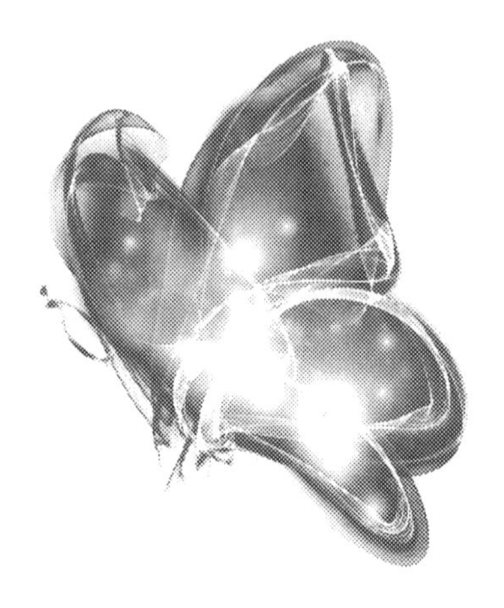

**We have a choice between grief and joy.**

women couldn't see the positive outcome, can *we* dare ask what good might come from death?

Certainly, we can dare to ask. We *should* dare to ask. Fr. Ken would want us to ask.

By choosing a human life, even if for a few days, Stephanie's soul experienced immense human love, founded in Linda and Ron's desire to birth and raise a third child. When we ask the deep questions, we realize that, like the rest of us, Stephanie's life began with no guarantee regarding the length of time she would live in a human body.

But, as you will soon see, this tiny infant child was a catalyst. Stephanie pushed us—even those of you who know her through the pages in this book—forward in our lives, in our capacity for *love,* in our *evolution.* Just look at those words. But now instead, look from an alternative perspective: *evolution* begins with e-v-o-l. Or: l-o-v-e!

"Unconditional love is the most powerful stimulant of the immune system," writes cancer surgeon Dr. Bernie Seigel in his book *Love, Medicine & Miracles: Lessons Learned about Self-Healing from a Surgeon's Experience with Exceptional Patients.* "The truth is: love heals," he says. "Miracles happen to exceptional patients every day—patients who have the courage to love, those who have the courage to work with their doctors to participate in and influence their own recovery." Maybe the band Roxy Music knew this when they wrote their song, *Love Is the Drug.*

In his book *Care of the Soul,* spiritual writer Thomas More says that physical symptoms are the voice of the soul, a way for us to talk to who we really are within our inner self and to find out what our soul really is. Maybe disease also has a purpose: to take my life from me; or, to wake me from the type of life I've been leading and, thus, help me move on to a bigger, better life with new perspective.

The common, initial reaction to illness and pain is to feel regret and heartache. Rare is the person who welcomes negative symptoms. But that's what poet and writer Mark Nepo did. In his book *Reduced to Joy,*

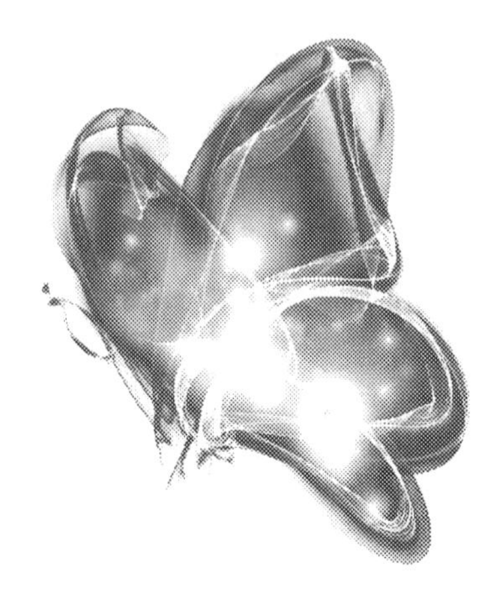

**Change the thought;
change the outcome.**

Nepo eloquently describes how he embraced the cancer that consumed three of his ribs and nearly killed him but also transformed him into someone who has touched the lives of many with meaning and purpose through his spoken and written words.

What is the purpose of a headache, if not to be hit over the head with the fact that something is causing stress and anxiety? What is the purpose of depression, but to remind us that we have a choice between grief and joy? What is the purpose of any disease, if not to make us ask: "Who am I? What am I here for?"

We can ask the disease: "What are you? Why did you enter my life? Who do you represent? What are you here for? What am I supposed to learn from you? What am I to do now?" In the end, we will find that it is up to us to create a culture of health with a new thought and life choices that might have seemed odd to our previous way of living.

Improve, get better is the message from any good coach. That's the connection with *Sportuality*: Change the thought; change the outcome.

Everything *does* have a purpose. Everything! Even a crucifixion, without which, there can be no resurrection.

And what is a resurrection? Physically, it's an overcoming or surmounting of death. Metaphysically, it's a reawakening or a rebirth. Mentally and emotionally, it's a changing of mind about the meaning of the world. According to Fr. Ken, it's a transformation.

For the Nartkers, Stephanie's death was the precursor to a series of profound transformations involving Linda, Ron, their biological children Courtney and Eric, and the unknown children they would come to adopt.

Yes, Linda and Ron did move forward after Stephanie's death as if they were following a script fueled by love and purpose. Why? Because they had a purpose larger than prolonged grief.

Who were they? The parents in the Nartker family.

What were they here for? To raise their children, all four of them. No, really, all five of them.

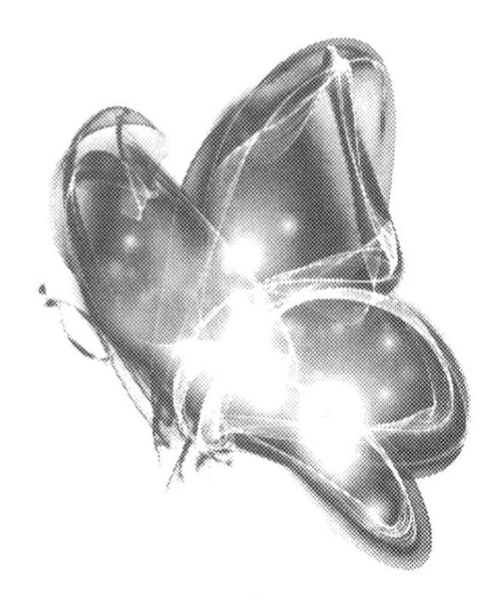

**What ailment or malady or tragedy is afflicting or has afflicted you?**

But to elaborate on that now would be to get ahead of the story. So, let's take a time out for reflection, then we'll lay some more foundation that will help us better understand Max—and who he is and what he's here for.

**TIME OUT**

What ailment or malady or tragedy is afflicting or has afflicted you? Can you go deep inside and, with sincerity and genuine desire to know, ask any malady or trauma or unsettling circumstance, "What are you? Why are you here in my life?"

Can you put yourself in the tiny preternatural mind of Stephanie and ask yourself: How would Stephanie answer the questions of "Who am I?" and "What am I here for ... even if only for a few days?" Can we really measure out love from the perspective of time?

Can you grasp the concept that Stephanie—and all of us—came from the Divine energy represented by the vertical beam on Christ's cross? That she lived—like all of us—in the horizontal Earth plane? And that her life—like the lives of all of us—represents the intersection of the Divine vertical and the human horizontal?

While challenging to accept, especially during the periods of tragedy, this concept is actually very freeing; it helps us answer and know, "Where's the good in this?"

**Everything of value in life—
love, peace, joy—exists in the Now.**

## CHAPTER 5

# In the Now

*"I cannot tell you any spiritual truth that deep within you don't know already. All I can do is remind you of what you have forgotten."*

**— Eckhart Tolle**

In his book *The Power of Now,* Eckhart Tolle implores us to embrace "the Now," the time and space where there is no regret, where failure does not exist, and where possibilities are endless.

In the Now, there is no wishing and hoping; there is only acceptance and moving forward … like Linda and Ron accepting Stephanie's death and moving forward with Eric's birthday celebration.

Max also spoke his first words to me in the present: "Who ARE you? What ARE you here for?" (Not in the past: "Who WERE you? What WERE you here for?" Nor in the future: "Who WILL you be? What WILL you be here for?")

Everything of value in life—love, peace, joy—exists in the Now. To imagine the past or the future is to invite the ghosts of recollection and the vagaries of conjecture. We have to remember the admonition that worry is praying for something we *don't* want.

One of my favorite, most simple prayers comes from spiritual author and speaker, Marianne Williamson, who proclaims, "Thank you for letting

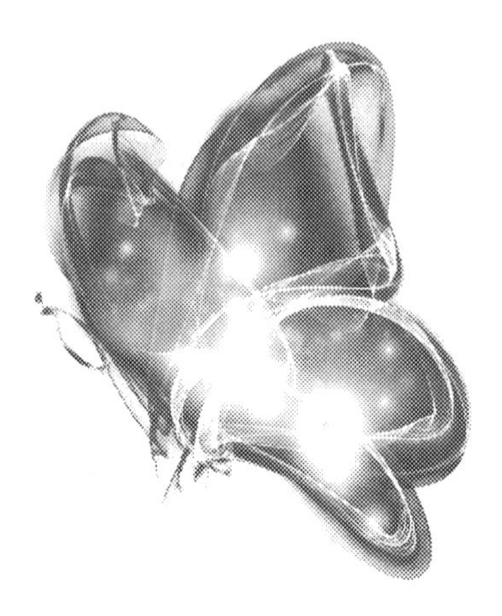

**We are part of the collective consciousness of all life.**

me know that everything is happening exactly as it should." Even when it appears not to be so in our cultural way of thinking.

The message from Linda and Ron—and from Max and Elena, as we shall see—is to live in this Now moment and, in each and every Now moment, to constantly and consistently affirm, "I choose love. I choose peace. I choose joy."

This is the Universal Message of Abraham, Mohammad, Christ, Buddha, as well as more recent and avatars such as Mahatma Gandhi, Eleanor Roosevelt, Nelson Mandela, Martin Luther King, Jr., The Dalai Lama, Mother Teresa, Bess Truman, Thich Nhat Hanh, Oprah Winfrey, and Aung San Suu Kyi. Their Universal Messages have always been part of humanity's collective consciousness but are only *now* becoming known by more and more people through an ever-growing human awareness and the miracle of social media. Thus, we are *now* beginning to *know* more about who we are and what we are here for … as individuals and as the collective whole.

Who are we? We are part of the collective consciousness of all life.

What are we here for? In my experience, the answer has to be "to love," and to experience love's ancillary cousins of peace, happiness, joy, bliss, and kindness.

I believe it's as simple as that. But think critically about that last statement—that our purpose is "to love." Is that merely my opinion? Is it a statement of fact, a universal truth as found in the sacred books? Is it a wish for all humanity? Or, just maybe, all of the above?

# THE POWER OF WORDS

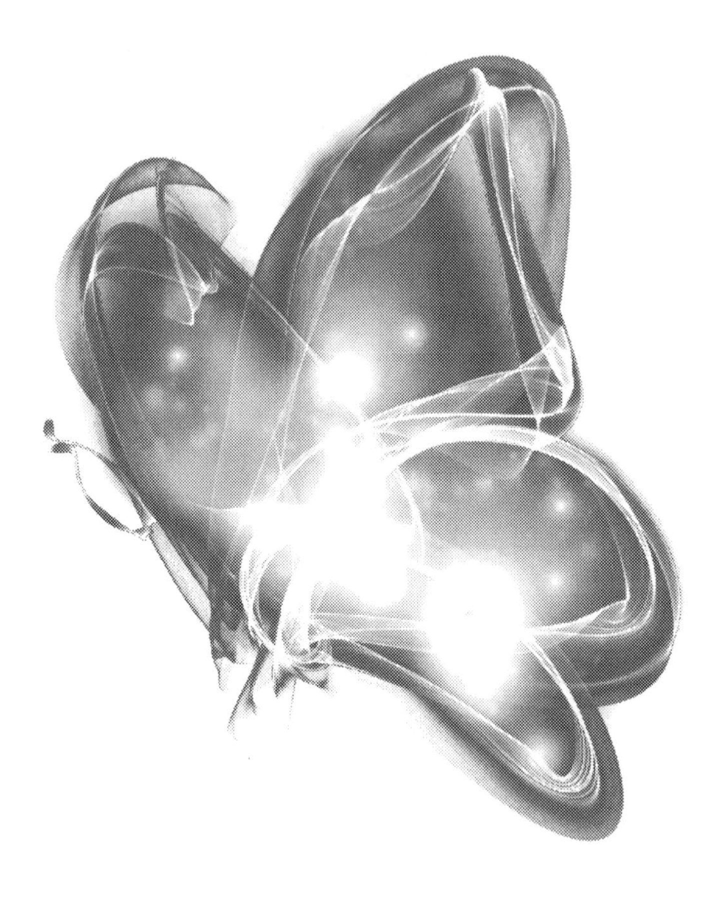

# THE POWER OF WORDS

Words have power. That power comes from our thoughts and intentions that lie behind the words. The main use of language, then, is to move thoughts and ideas from one mind to another—from yours to mine, from mine to yours. As we do that, we transform ourselves into a non-physical dimension of communication.

Interestingly, none of the words that Max spoke on that fateful day—"Who are you? What are you here for"—is over four characters in length. Yet, their succinctness carries tremendous weight, if taken in the context of sportuality and conscious thought.

For, you see, through his words to me on that first day of our relationship, Max communicated so much more to me than asking simple questions. His language was an expression of his inner self. But, unfortunately, for many of us, there exists certain limitations among language, and humans often struggle to express all that they think.

I wrote about this in my first book, *Sportuality: Finding Joy in the Games* in which I examined the definition of words commonly used in sport: competition, spirit, enthusiasm, victory, communication, community, education, humor, holy, religion, sanctuary, and sacrifice. I pointed out how they had been corrupted by society and tradition away from their original positive etymology, often to the point of presenting quite an opposite negative, aggressive message. I presented the idea that, by holding in our minds a different thought about our words, we can attain a great difference in our lived outcome. In our minds, then, we can literally and physically move from pain to joy, from hate to love, from war to peace.

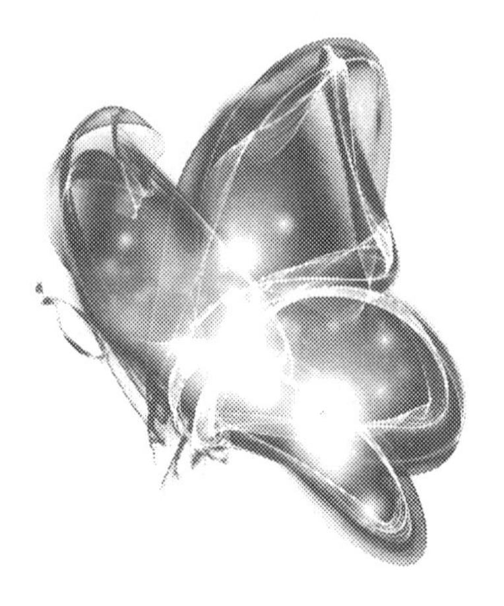

***I am*** **so much more than the sum of my parts.**

# CHAPTER 6

## Who Are *You,* Max?

*"In the beginning was the Word."*

**—John 1:1**

As hard as I might try to compartmentalize the pieces of my life, it is quite clear that none of the societal roles I play—daughter, sister, coach, wife, mother, mother-in-law, friend, author, and now grandmother—are separate or distinct from the others. *I am* so much more than the sum of my parts.

Through the words of many modern metaphysical writers, such as Dr. Wayne Dyer, people have become highly conscious of the power behind the words "I am,"—whether spoken or thought—to create either undesirable or desirable outcomes. "I am sick" leads to or worsens sickness. "I am happy" augments the state of happiness.

But the power of "I am" is not new. In the Old Testament, Moses and God, manifested as a burning bush, have a "what are you here for" conversation in which God says to Moses, "Go to Pharaoh and bring my people, the Israelites, out of Egypt." When Moses asks, "Who should I say has sent me?" God answers, "I Am who I Am. Say that 'I Am has sent me.'"

Max's first words to me have generated a great awareness of the power of the words that follow "I am."

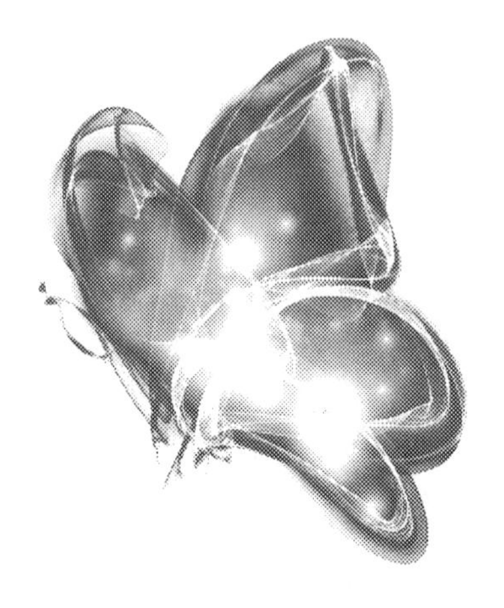

**"I'm going to be the next Ernie Harwell."**

Who am I? "*I am* a daughter, sister, coach, wife, mother, mother-in-law, friend, author, grandmother—and more."

What am I here for? "*I am* here to be an expression of love and joy to all these people."

Did I realize all of who I am when Max asserted his hard questions? Yes, at some subconscious level. Did I reply with awareness of that concept (like I would today)? No, of course not. I wasn't yet ready or able to at that point in my life. So I answered in the usual manner with my name, my job, and my purpose for attending the game … and sitting where I sat. I answered from my ego.

It wasn't until several months later, after Max's questions had swum around in the sea of my life, that their impact began to hit me. After all, these are questions that never really go away. So, I turned the tables on him, and asked, "Who are *you,* Max? What are *you* here for?" In a heartbeat, he replied, "I'm going to be the next Ernie Harwell," a reference to his love for baseball and admiration for the great Hall of Fame broadcaster of the Detroit Tigers professional baseball team.

Again, Max's words buzzed me like a stinging hornet, but in a good way. Ernie Harwell. God, I love that man. He was the voice of my childhood who opened the door into a lifelong love of baseball. And then to have watched my two sons play for the Tigers' organization was, for me, a dream come true. My oldest son even attended the game at Comerica Park where Ernie, in the latter days of his life, said good bye to the fans, the club, and the city. Ernie was, indeed, a rare individual. So when Max, another emerging rare individual life, stated his life goal as being the *next* Ernie, I heard his words and my consciousness took note.

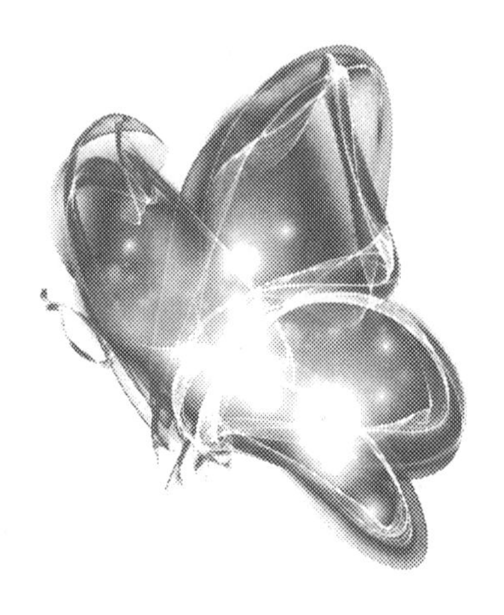

**"In baseball, democracy shines its clearest. Here the only race that matters is the race to the bag."**

## CHAPTER 7

# Ernie

*"I look on life as a joyous adventure."*

**— Ernie Harwell**

When it comes to sportual heroes, none compare with a sports icon whose image on the Internet could have any number of hashtags: baseball, faithful, devoted husband, committed, memorable, legendary, Detroit Tigers, dulcet voice, storyteller, gentleman, gentle man.

As a child, I would fall asleep with my transistor radio under my pillow, listening to this man's melodic voice calling baseball play-by-play. He is so iconic, so revered, that we need only say his first name—like Elvis, Bono, Cher, Oprah, or Madonna.

Ernie.

For those who need further explanation: Ernie Harwell (1918 – 2010), Hall of Fame broadcaster for the Detroit Tigers baseball team from 1960 to 1991 and 1993 to 2002.

Ernie broadcast professional baseball games for 55 seasons, mostly with the Tigers but also with the Atlanta [Georgia] Crackers, Brooklyn Dodgers, New York Yankees, Baltimore Orioles, and California Angels. He called the play-by-play at All-Star games and the World Series for NBC Radio, league and divisional championship games for CBS Radio and ESPN Radio, and the Game of the Week on CBS Radio. He enjoyed

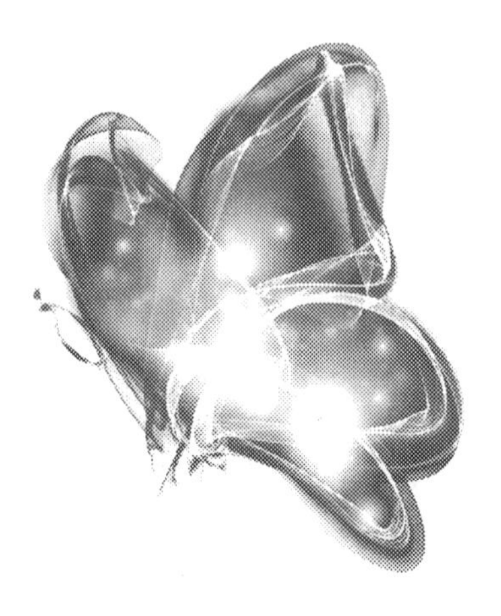

**"If baseball could talk, it would sound like Ernie Harwell."**

numerous cameo guest celebrity broadcast appearances, including as a color commentator for Fox Sports Network Detroit television.

Ernie made stories real. His poignant essay, "The Game for All America," published in *The Sporting News* in 1955 and reprinted numerous times since, is a classic in baseball literature.

> "... Baseball is a spirited race of man against man, reflex against reflex. A game of inches. Every skill is measured. Every heroic, every failing is seen and cheered—or booed. And then becomes a statistic.
>
> In baseball, democracy shines its clearest. Here the only race that matters is the race to the bag. The creed is the rule book. Color is something to distinguish one team's uniform from another. ..."

Ernie wrote popular songs, quipping, "I have more no-hitters than Nolan Ryan." He made cameo appearances in made-for-television movies and one film, *Cobb,* about baseball great Ty Cobb, and his voice is heard as part of the soundtrack in three other films.

He penned columns for the *Detroit Free Press* newspaper and authored several books on baseball. He was the subject of many volumes by others, including a documentary by the *Detroit Free Press* and the nostalgic stage play *Ernie* by famous Detroit writer Mitch Albom, who quipped, "If baseball could talk, it would sound like Ernie Harwell."

Named Michigan Sportscaster of the Year 19 times, he is an inductee of the National Sportscasters and Sportswriters Association Hall of Fame, the American Sportscasters Association Hall of Fame, the Baseball Hall of Fame, the Michigan Sports Hall of Fame, the National Radio Hall of Fame, and the Georgia Sports Hall of Fame.

The press box at the Detroit Tigers home field, Comerica Park, is officially named the Ernie Harwell Media Center. The Cleveland Indians

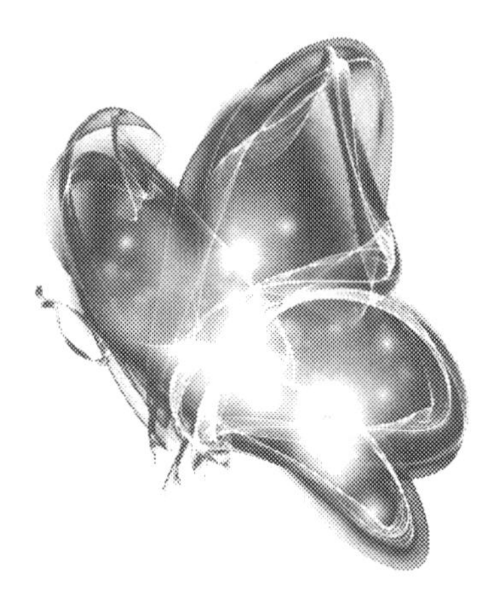

**Ernie. Is. Legend.**

baseball team honored him by naming their visiting team radio booth at Progressive Field the Ernie Harwell Visiting Radio Booth. The former home field site of the Detroit Tigers, Tiger Stadium, is unofficially known as Ernie Harwell Park. A room at the Detroit Public Library honors both Ernie and his wife, Lulu, who wed in 1941 and were married for 68 years. And Detroit's Wayne State University has constructed a new baseball stadium, called Harwell Field, that also pays tribute to the Harwells.

For those of you who knew all of this about Ernie already, we can simply affirm: Ernie. Is. Legend.

Legend!

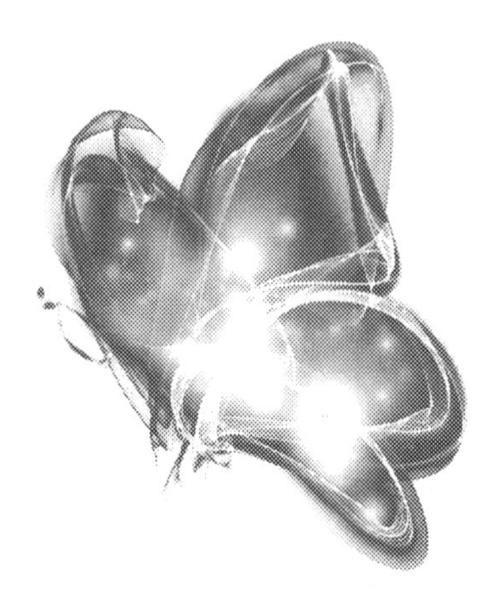

**Ernie Harwell was a transformational presence in the lives of baseball and non-baseball people alike.**

# CHAPTER 8

# Legend

*"Given a choice of being right or being kind,*
*it's better to be kind."*

**— Ernie Harwell**

The word "legend" hails from the Middle English *legende*, which means "the written account of a saint's life." I like that. Saint Ernie.

So, yes, by saying that Ernie is legend, I'm also saying that Ernie is a saint. This isn't a concept that applies only to Ernie Harwell; it applies to so many other people too … sports heroes and heroes in other endeavors. Babe Ruth. Babe Didrikson Zaharias. Mohammad Ali. Knute Rockne. Billie Jean King. Flo Hyman. John Wooden. Shakespeare. Mozart. Einstein. Oh, and so many more.

What do we know of these legendary people? Some acted like saints and others did not. Some were eccentric and some were more ordinary. In their daily lives, they were different. Each of their endeavors was unique.

We can only surmise as to whether or not they asked themselves the foundational questions of "Who are you?" and "What are you here for?" in those precise words. But we can tell by their accomplishments that theirs were lives of great impact. At some level of consciousness, they possessed the foundational characteristic of knowing they were significant

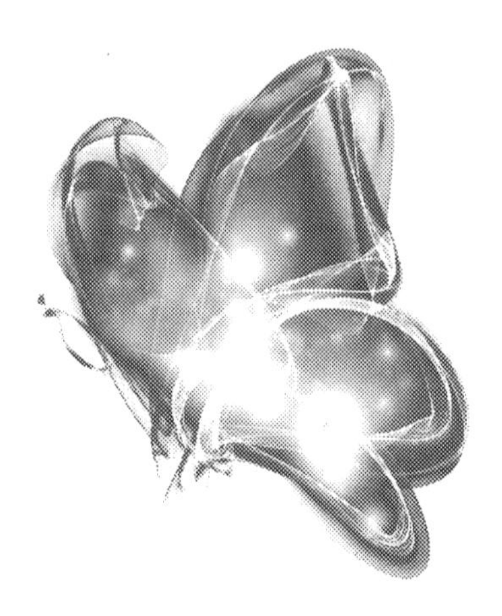

**“Everyone who tries to be like Ernie is somehow the better for it.”**

and their accomplishments were above the norm. They must have had some inner impetus to use their minds and bodies and talents *to the max* for the higher and greater good of all.

Looking beyond his awards and honors, his legendary status and his induction into every hall of fame for which he was eligible, Ernie Harwell was a transformational presence in the lives of baseball and non-baseball people alike. He had the unique ability to take the game of baseball, with all its special nuances, and turn it into a magical, meaningful, and purposeful experience in the ears and minds of radio listeners. With his deeply ethical, Christian belief, he probably evangelized more people into the religion of baseball than did Babe Ruth, Joe DiMaggio, Mickey Mantle, and Derek Jeter combined.

In an article in the *Detroit Free Press* after Ernie's death on May 6, 2010, Mitch Albom described him as "unhurried, slightly southern, as comfortable as an old couch." Albom also penned what made Ernie "Ernie":

> "... Harwell was so much more than an announcer. He was a voice inside all of us as well as outside of us. A voice you can still hear, even though the world has silenced it. He was a man to admire, a satisfied soul, a shining example of a life lived purely and honestly. And because of that, Ernie will live on inside everyone who ever met him, shook his hand, gave him a hug, or simply heard his soothing words come through a tiny speaker in a car radio, or through an earphone hidden from the teacher on a school day afternoon."

In another article for the *Detroit Free Press,* Albom quotes actor Peter Cary, who transforms into Ernie in Albom's stage play, *Ernie,* "It's such an honor to play Ernie, and to see how people react. Many of them have tears in their eyes."

Then Albom adds the ultimate tribute statement. "... after six years of performances like Carey's, one thing seems obvious: Everyone who tries to be like Ernie is somehow the better for it."

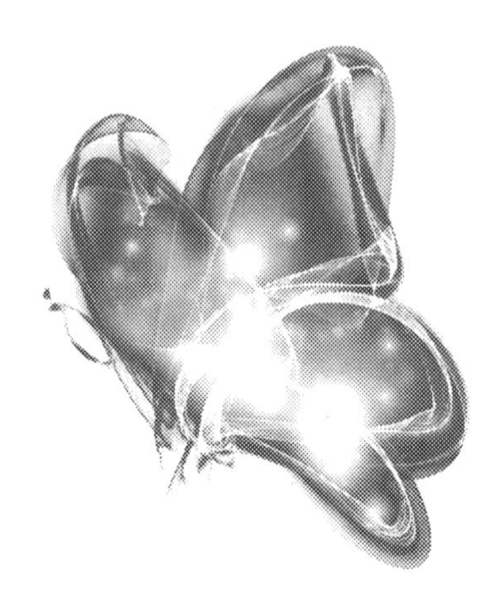

**"I'm here to accept God's will and to do God's work, to live my dream as a professional communicator, to tell the story of others and let my story also be told."**

Re-enter Max's goal, "I want to be the next Ernie Harwell!"

What? Really? What a brash statement for a kid from Midwest America who has challenges with anxiety, ADHD, and spectrum disorder and who unabashedly speaks without what others might view as "socially acceptable filters."

But he does know baseball and most other sports inside and out; in truth, he's a walking encyclopedia of sports knowledge, including the trivial. While other announcers might draw upon decades of personal experience and a research department with computer databases in hand to provide them with live game-time patter, Max, as a teenager, has all of that already in his head.

So, why not? Why can't or shouldn't Max be the next Ernie Harwell? Or an announcer like Ernie Harwell? Whether he does or not is simply a matter of belief … and spirit.

"Well, what about those social skills, or the absence of them?" some people might say. "What about coming across too caustically, like with his finger-pointing, forehead-thumping questions, 'Who are you?' and 'What are you here for?'"

Yes, well, those are hurdles, but they can be overcome; they are not show-stoppers.

Therefore, I ask in return, "What about the fact that Ernie Harwell, when a boy, stuttered?" Yes, the dulcet-toned Voice of the Detroit Tigers, who so many came to know and love and admire, spoke with a severe stutter as well as a lisp as a youngster. How many people, like those who might chastise Max, might have said, "Oh, Ernie, you can never be an announcer; you don't talk right."

Did Ernie listen? We don't know. But probably, he ignored those who would attempt to limit him. Or maybe he listened enough to decide, "Because I want to be an announcer, I will have to overcome this disability." Maybe he listened enough to draw upon his own self-induced determination to seek teacher-assisted training to overcome that speech impediment and, thus, gain *his* maxAbility.

Who are you, Ernie Harwell? What are you here for?

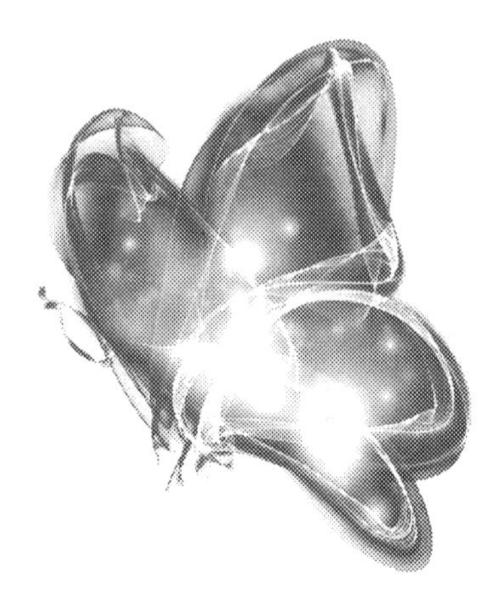

**What was once "bad" is now "good."**

Perhaps, back then, Ernie might have answered: "I'm a kid with a speech impediment." With an inkling that would lead to the fervor of a saint and the makings of a spiritual legend deep within, perhaps he confided to himself, "But I'm here to accept God's will and to do God's work, to live my dream as a professional communicator, to tell the story of others and let my story also be told."

As Max grew into a more mature high school teen and then a responsible adult college student, he began to ask his provocative questions with greater gentleness and courtesy. Claiming his destiny, he queried himself: "Who am I? What am I here for?" Often, he would answer, "To tell people about Jesus."

Overcoming a speaking difficulty—whether to be a play-by-play announcer or an evangelist or a teacher or a relationship partner and member of a functioning family—is a challenge. It's one of those situations in which the harder you try the more difficult the challenge can become. Nervousness and anxiety are huge impact factors. And fear breeds failure.

One of my students at Kalamazoo College used to stutter so badly that she decided to attend a conference on stuttering. Because the conference was several hundred miles away, she flew ... and was stopped at the security checkpoint of a major airport because she couldn't speak well enough to answer the TSA agent's questions. In a hurry to catch her plane, her anxiety exacerbated the situation into hopeless frustration. Today, she carries a card that, when necessary, explains her condition, a card that she has made available to other stutterers throughout the country.

She also began to practice yoga as a calming exercise and even wrote her senior project on this subject. She has since used that academic work as a foundation for her professional career of helping others overcome speech impediments.

For her, what was once "bad" is now "good." Out of her frightening situation at the airport, she emerged as an advocate for others with speech difficulties. Within her "deathly" terror, she found her resurrection. And the inspiration to help others. In the spirit of love and service, she rose out of her pain to transform challenge into opportunity.

**Ernie simply followed what his heart told him to do and went where his gifts led him to be.**

In *Sportuality,* I defined the word communication according to its etymological roots, which is the Latin *communicare,* "to impart, to make common." Today, we use the word to indicate imparting knowledge; to make known; to give, express, or interchange thoughts, feelings, and information by writing or speaking.

Consider those definitions applied to a person with a speech impediment. Imagine yourself as my former student trying to impart knowledge of her condition, thoughts, and feelings to the security agent at that busy international airport. Can you feel her frustration? Can you feel the agent's frustration?

Without the ability to communicate, to *make common* their individual purposes, the situation for my student and that security agent became hopelessly entangled in *mis*-communication.

As I write this chapter, pitchers and catchers are reporting to baseball's spring training in Florida and Arizona. They will learn and practice the language of their sport: silent hand signals from catcher to pitcher, from coach to batters and runners, from manager to position players on the field. Each set of signals is unique to each team but common to all the players on a team.

Spring training is also the glorious event that marks the beginning of the annual baseball season when the Boys of Summer come out to play America's Game.

Each spring, for his initial broadcast, Ernie would invoke words from the Bible, the Song of Solomon, chapter 2, verses 11 and 12:

> For, lo, the winter is past,
> The rain is over and gone;
> The flowers appear on the earth;
> The time of the singing of birds is come,
> And the voice of the turtle is heard in our land.

Ernie's themes of winter and spring, of death and rebirth, of faith and hope, and of joy in the game—lo, even of resurrection—epitomized the

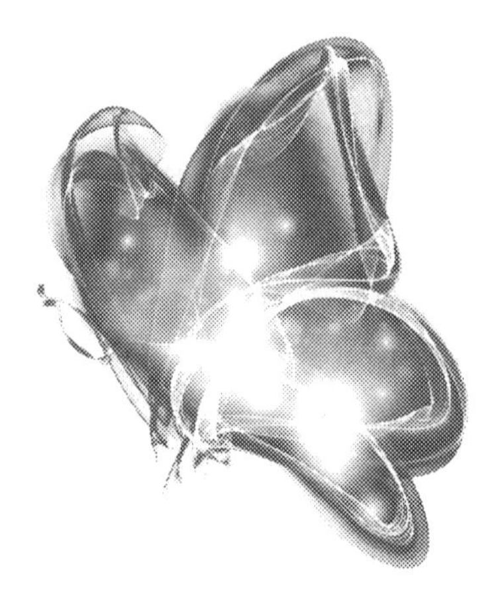

# Ernie: how a person should be!

man who Ernie was. Not only a hall of fame broadcaster but one of the most sportual men to have graced us with his vocal gifts.

I'm going to go out on a limb here and say that Ernie never set out to be a legend. Ernie simply followed what his heart told him to do and went where his gifts led him to be. He simply followed the path of least resistance to the career of his dreams. His daily life answered the questions: "Who am I? What am I here for?"

As he said in his farewell address at Comerica Park on September 17, 2009, "In my almost 92 years on this Earth, the good Lord has blessed me with a great journey." And this sentiment was punctuated by the words on a sign, held aloft by a fan that day: "How a person should be!"

That's Ernie: how a person should be!

**TIME OUT**

Ernie Harwell was a communicator. So are you. How do you use communication—or might you use greater communication—to create a commonness, a common bond, with others? What is your preferred method of communication?

Who are some of your sportual heroes, your legends, and why do they resonate within you? How do you think they—or Ernie—would have answered the questions: "Who am you? What are you here for?"

**You are becoming whole and healed by choosing to follow your heart's desire.**

# CHAPTER 9

# Enthusiasm

*"You can do anything if you have enthusiasm."*

**— Henry Ford**

My book *Sportuality* defines the related words *enthuse* and *enthusiasm* according to their Greek and Latin etymology as "having a god within." *En* for "in" or "within." *Theos* (*thus*) for god.

To meet and to know Max is to know that he very enthusiastically carries his "God within" visibly on his shirt sleeves. It is impossible to have an interaction with Max and not be affected and become enthusiastic yourself. You will know his God, his enlivening energy, his faith. Just like Ernie, who often affirmed his Christian values.

So, can Max be a great sports announcer? Can he be the next Ernie Harwell? No one who meets him doubts the possibility. Max's "God within" shines forth through his love of family, his love of baseball, his faith, and his magnetic personality that enables him to connect so well with his fellow humans. All attributes that he shares with Ernie.

But, as often happens, plans change. As we learned earlier, new ideas emerge. What Max is now choosing to "do" is different, but who he "is" has remained the same. And, regardless of what he does, Max is and will still be Max.

**We are one with the Creator just as we are one with all other humans and all other creatures.**

My story is similar. I went to school at the University of Michigan with intention of becoming a doctor, but, instead, I became a professor and coach. I can't tell you how many times I've had a conversation with a student who matriculated to Kalamazoo College with the intention to study pre-med only to realize that their real passion lies elsewhere. The conversation is always about the struggle to leave the original dream behind in favor of a new dream. My advice is always this: "You are becoming whole and healed by choosing to follow your heart's desire."

That is real education, which etymologically means "to draw forth." When a student knows their heart and has the courage to follow where it leads, they are well on the way to living a life of purpose and joy.

Because of his faith and his energy, Max has affirmed my faith that anything is possible. And for that, *I am* enthusiastically grateful.

Max and I recently had a conversation in which he apologized to me in advance of sharing the news that he wasn't going to be the next Ernie Harwell. He had decided, instead, to spread the love and joy of God through the spoken word. It didn't take me long to let him know that that is *exactly* what Ernie did.

Thus, Max reminded me to ask our thematic questions from a spiritual perspective: Who are we in regard to our relationship with God? We are one with the Creator just as we are one with all other humans and all other creatures.

What are we here for? To be enthused with life. To find our "God-Within."

**TIME OUT**

How many times have you said, "I am going to be/do..."? How did you see yourself becoming or achieving that? Could you feel the reality? Did you become who you set out to be? Why? Or why not?

What a beautiful awareness when we can know what we do or who we become is first created in the mind.

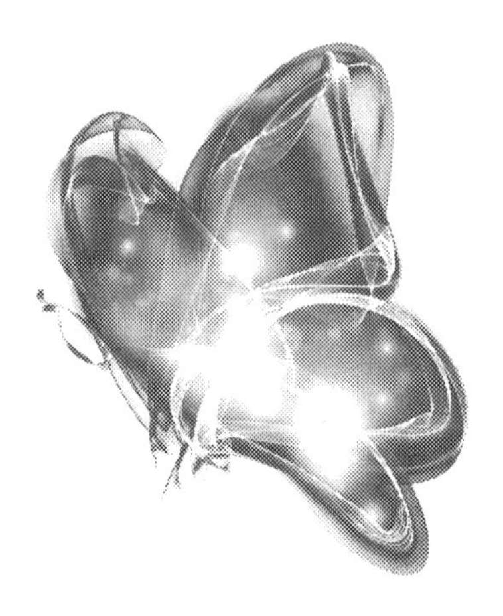

**Max is no ordinary young man.**

## CHAPTER 10

# Max and Jim

When Courtney decided to attend Kalamazoo College as a student-athlete on our volleyball team, I was excited. But knew I was going to have to win Max over. Not only was his big sister and oldest sibling leaving home to go to a college, Max was still vocal about her being three hours away and playing on a team of "things that sting."

Enter Jim, my wonderful, athletic, sportual husband.

The summer before Courtney's matriculation, the older of our two sons was playing for the Detroit Tigers' Class A team, the Whitecaps, in Grand Rapids, Michigan. The Loons, another professional minor league team affiliated with the Los Angeles Dodgers, played its home games at Dow Diamond, not far from where the Nartkers live. So Jim and I decided that it would be fun to connect with the Nartker family at a White Caps-Loons game in Midland.

Linda and Ron, my future volleyball setter Courtney, Eric, Max, and Elena were seated on a blanket on a grassy berm beyond the right field home run fence when we arrived. Max greeted Jim as though they were long-lost buddies with as much forward thrust as he had confronted me, but in a more *mano a mano* manner. The two went for a walk around the stadium's concourse, and Jim quickly saw what I had long ago perceived: Max is no ordinary young man.

Max knew everyone, and talked continuously to either Jim or the many people who greeted him. "It was like a parade, and he was the grand marshal!" Jim exclaimed later.

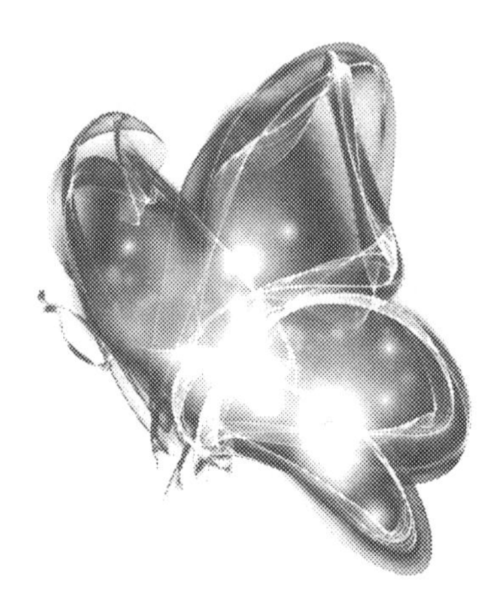

**For, you see, Max and Elena are adopted.**

Jim and Max bonded immediately, sharing stories, jokes, and magic tricks. I sensed that the youth, still a middle school student, was beginning to make peace with Courtney's decision. But I also knew that Linda and Ron had a lot of work to do to maintain constancy within their changing family dynamic.

Courtney's departure was, in a way, like Stephanie's life-ending departure. And Max and Elena's arrival on the scene, less than a year after Stephanie's death, wasn't without both tremendous joys and upheavals. For, you see, Max and Elena are adopted.

# THE POWER OF LOVE

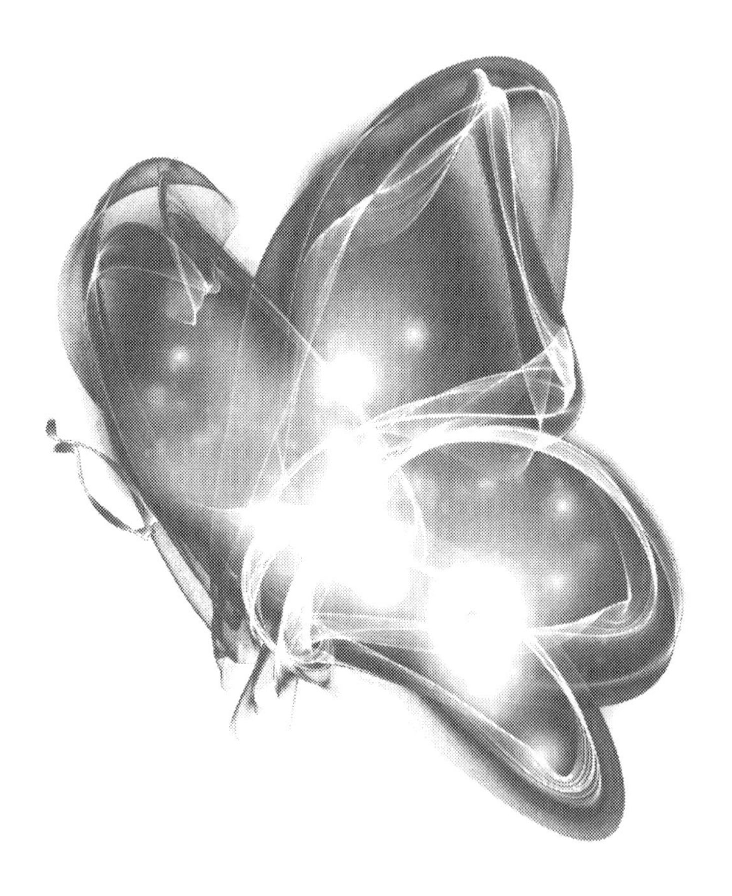

# THE POWER OF LOVE

As I write this page, Valentine's Day falls during the coming week. Days like this tell us that love is something we could commodify and commercialize: buy a card, buy gifts, buy candy and flowers to show another the depth of our love. But that makes love a physical entity, when in fact, love is more spiritual, more emotional, and even more mental than physical.

This section about the power of Love (yes, that's with a capital "L") is about the Nartker's spiritual, emotional, and mental journey toward Max and Elena. I believe, in my miracle-minded thinking, that they journeyed from the heart, in Love, toward one another. I believe that all families seeking adoption do the same. While that Love that brought them together provides a physical home and physical care, adoption—or the intention to adopt—is an outcome of the Spirit.

Sometimes Spirit breathes gently into our thoughts. Sometimes we envision Spirit through our dreams. And sometimes Spirit screams at the top of its lungs out of grief. The story of Linda and Ron Nartker's road to Russia, where Max and Elena entered the Earth plane, is one of Love. True, Spiritual Love.

Their love embodies the spirit in I Corinthians 13:4-7, New International Version: "Love is patient. Love is kind. It does not envy. It does not boast. It is not proud. It does not dishonor others. It is not self-seeking. It is not easily angered. It keeps no record of wrongs. Love does not delight in evil but rejoices with the truth. It always protects, always trusts, always hopes, always perseveres."

With this as our definition of Love, there is never a guarantee that our path will be easy or perfect or seamless. Often it is not, but Love perseveres. Just like Ron and Linda in their journey, from Michigan to Russia, toward a complete family, their story exposes Love, and it connects us with each other in Love.

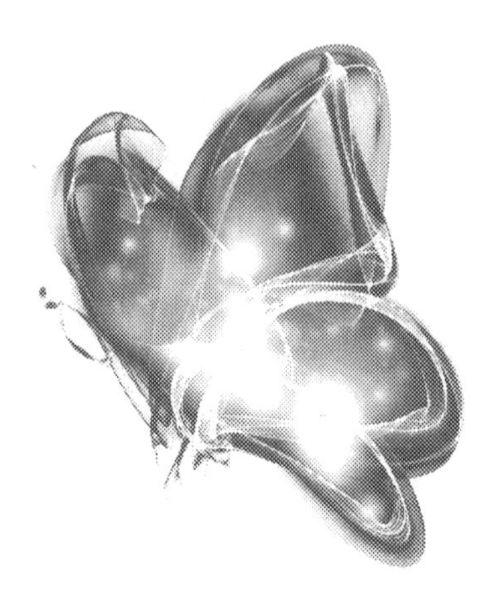

**Anything is possible [when on]**
**a mission of love, of desire,**
**of knowing, of trust**

# CHAPTER 11

# Russia

*"Nothing will happen in your life unless you try something."*

**—Russian Proverb**

In the decades before and after World War II, the United States government labeled Russia, with its Communist political system, an enemy and, through propaganda, sold that concept to the US population. Meekly and without thinking, many people went along with the idea that Russians were a menace to be feared. Those who protested against the idea that Russia and Russians were evil were labeled as "un-American," perpetuating an "us-versus-them" paradigm.

In politics today, Russia is still viewed as a detrimental influence on American politics; its leaders suspected of even tampering with recent US elections. Whether the Russian government or individuals within Russia did or did not tamper is not my issue here. What I oppose is the judging and labeling of all people within a country—our country or another country—by the actions of a few. I oppose the propaganda machines—of our country or any other country—that prey on fear.

I prefer love, acceptance, peace, and joy as demonstrated by Ron and Linda through international adoption.

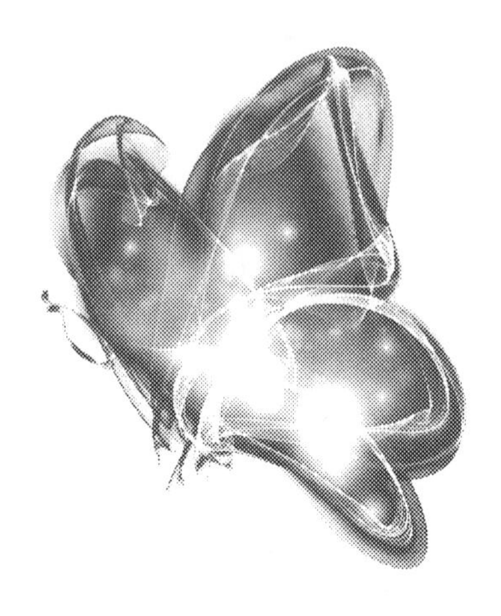

**Max . . . is on a mission.**
**He knows what he wants.**
**And he knows when he has connected**
**with what he wants.**

And that relates to Max and Elena, children born in Russia who are now part of a healthy and wonderful US family. Their journey from Russia to here, carried by Love through the dark veil of propagandist mentality of the 1990s, indicates that "anything is possible."

Indeed, Max exhibits that "anything is possible" attitude in all possible ways. Some of his propensity for optimism, as we shall see, comes from within Max himself. But his parents, Ron and Linda Nartker, also deserve credit for instilling that mindset in all of their children. How do they instill that sense of optimism and perfection? Through their own actions.

The Nartkers' story of adoption is an epic journey. It's a mission of love, of desire, of knowing, of trust.

Their philosophy of moving forward, regardless of the obstacles, even when dealing with a foreign country that some Americans still fear, fits their match with Max perfectly. Why? Because Max never stops moving. He's on a mission. He knows what he wants. And he knows when he has connected with what he wants.

He knows who he is and what he's here for.

In his book *Memories of Heaven: Children's Astounding Recollections of the Time Before They Came to Earth*, author Wayne Dyer makes this idea perfectly clear. Adopted children, he writes, relate thoughts of seeing and choosing their adoptive parents before their incarnation, of knowing they must go through another channel (biological birth parents) to reach their future family, their destination.

The power of Universal Love, which is so much more forceful than hatred and bigotry, brought Max and Elena to the rest of their adoptive family.

When I think of the Nartkers, I see six of them: Ron and Linda, Courtney, Eric, Max and Elena. Because I was a late-comer to the Nartker party, I originally saw them through a glass darkly. I understood them only from the perspective of when and where I met them. I didn't have their history … then. Now, I do. And I see that Stephanie, though deceased, is still the seventh member of the Nartker family!

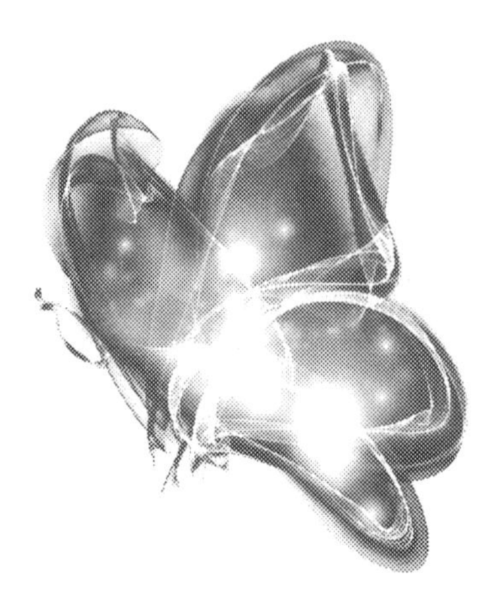

**"Judge not, lest ye be judged."**

In a way, her death was the spark that led Ron and Linda to adopt Russian children … as we shall see a few pages later.

But first …

**TIME OUT**

Spend some time in silence. Bring to mind and shine a light on a situation in which you might not have—or might not have had—the full picture. Think about how you originally judged that situation. As you reflect back, can you hold the all-inclusive, all-Loving "both-and" perspective of that situation in your mind? Can you see the situation with only Love? Can you think more expansively, without judgment, now?

Admittedly, it's hard to resist judgment. Or is it? Perhaps, through your own experiences with Love, you are seeing that it's becoming easier to choose oneness instead of separation? Perhaps Christ's admonition in the Bible, "Judge not, lest ye be judged," is becoming or has become a stronger inspiration to be fully accepting and, thus, not create separation and division by marginalizing some people as "inferior" or "enemies" or labeling them as "others."

**I see Max and Elena for who they are:**
**Children of the Universe.**
**They are, thus, *our children* too.**

## CHAPTER 12

# A Pregnancy of Paperwork

*"I didn't give you the gift of life. Life gave me the gift of you."*

**— unknown**

Max and Elena, from Russia, are two children whom I and many others have come to know and love as delightful, energetic, enthusiastic, contributing American citizens. They have been welcomed and incorporated well into an American family and an American community.

For me, personally, I know that, if I had entertained thoughts about people from Russia as being "others" or "enemies" or less than me, *I would be less.*

From my knowledge of the Nartker family, I see Max and Elena for who they are: Children of the Universe. They are, thus, *our children* too.

And the story of how they became part of the total American family, the American fabric of life, is remarkable.

Read now Linda's words and see the interwoven thread of oneness, connection, and healing. Perhaps you, like me, will be healed in some way from some past trauma.

> Even after we lost Stephanie, Ron and I still wanted a larger family. We decided to look into adoption. We researched adoption agencies and spoke with adoptive families. Then,

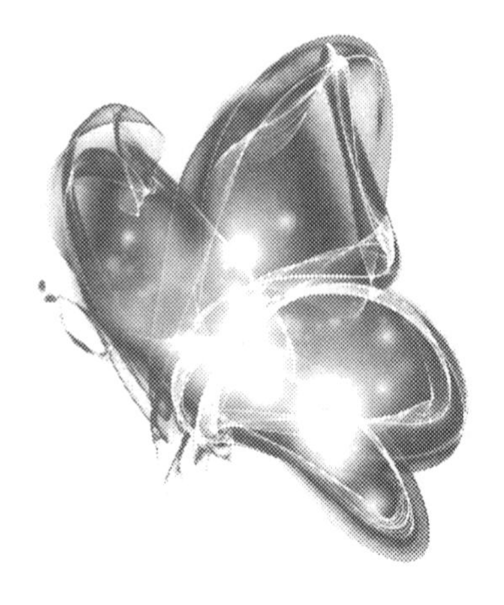

**Most of the [Russian] children were "social orphans" . . . let go by living parents.**

nearly a year after our baby's death, we were told of a news article about a family in my home town who had recently adopted two three-year-old girls from Russia, Tanya and Julia. After reading their story, we felt a pull to find out more, so we called the family and learned of their experience directly from them. We were fascinated!

I researched the adoption agency who had assisted them and found that their next international meeting would be in Columbus, Ohio, on that same weekend, September 13, 1997—my birthday. I made the five-hour drive on my own while Ron took Courtney and Eric to a family birthday party. He made up an excuse for my absence because we had chosen not to tell our family about our decision to adopt until we were certain it could and would happen.

I learned that the Ministry of Education in Moscow was responsible for all adoptions of Russian children and that we would need to travel to Russia in order to adopt. The trip could be as short as seven days or as long as two-and-a-half weeks if the "mandatory" ten-day waiting period was enforced, which it sometimes wasn't. Adoptions were completed in the region of the orphanage but final approval for visas and arrangements for the children's departure from Russia were granted in Moscow.

I and others at the meeting were told that more boys were available for adoption than girls because, in the Russian culture, girls were expected to care for their parents in old age. Most of the children were "social orphans," some of them abandoned in the birth hospital but many let go by living parents because of family disabilities, illness, or poverty with the intention that the parents would retrieve them later.

These "orphans" were listed in a national database for a minimum of three months to give Russian families

**A parent doesn't replace a lost child with another, or even two children. . . .**

priority before making them available for international adoption.

All children who were to enter an orphanage were quarantined in the birth hospital for six months to prevent them from carrying a contagious illness into the orphanage.

While the adoption agency hosted this gathering, some of the people there were adoptive American parents who brought their Russian children. After meeting them and hearing their stories, I drove back to Midland certain that their path would also become our path.

With the full knowledge of Courtney and Eric, Ron and I completed the initial paperwork: an application to the adoption agency, a petition to the US Immigration Services to rule on our suitability to adopt a foreign-born child, fingerprinting for criminal record background checks, and initiation of a home study by a local licensed adoption agency to confirm that our house was suitable and safe for children.

That was just the beginning! Over the next several months, we collected and submitted multiple copies of our birth certificates, marriage license, financial statements, tax forms, employment verification, medical histories, complete family histories, proof of insurances, our passports, and the deed to our house. Most of the documents needed to be notarized and then given an Apostille stamp, an international form of notarization by the State of Michigan in order to be legally recognized in Russia. And everything had to be translated into Russian!

We submitted so many documents that we came to know our FedEx courier by name.

Seeing the cost of obtaining, copying, and mailing these documents, we cut back on discretionary purchases and saved as much money as we could, knowing all the while, that these costs were also just the beginning.

**I relied on the strength I had gained from birthing and losing Stephanie.**

Our home study consisted of individual and joint interviews with Ron, me, and our children, as well as letters of reference to attest to our ability to parent adopted children and to maintain stable employment, and finally a home inspection.

Ron and I completed training for infant and child CPR.

Throughout the interview process, we were questioned about our own childhoods, our family life, our marriage, our biological children, our home life now, our faith, our parenting style, and, most importantly, our motivation for wanting to adopt.

"Are you using adoption to minimize or distract yourselves from grieving the loss of your infant daughter?" How insane, I thought. A parent doesn't replace a lost child with another or even two, children, even if they come from a nation across the ocean. Yet, I saw the validity of their question. "No," I answered. And I truly believed that we had moved beyond our grief of more than a year earlier, that we were now fully engaged in the "pregnancy of paperwork" involved with gestating two already-alive children we hadn't met yet. At the same time, I secretly acknowledged that Stephanie—her birth, life, and death—was the initial impetus for our dedication to this new way of bringing more children into our home.

"Do you understand the challenges with a foreign adoption? Do you understand that the children you adopt may have undiagnosed medical or emotional conditions that you won't discover until you bring them home?" Again, I relied on the strength I had gained from birthing and losing Stephanie. If I could handle the wrenching emotions of my experience with her, I could certainly deal with "undiagnosed conditions" of *living* children. "Yes, we understand."

In the end, we were deemed "emotionally stable."

No kidding!

**No matter which path you choose,
you are being true to your higher self.
Be grateful.**

**TIME OUT**

When pregnant with a wanted child, the expectant mother and father proceed day by day in the preparation for the birth. When adopting, the adopting parents can choose to abort at any time, on any day; they can simply walk away from the process.

Whether birthing or adopting, parents must know that they are also adopting a new lifestyle, they are inviting change and evolution.

If you were Linda and Ron, what would you do? Would you have the strength to walk daily through the seemingly endless interviews and applications? Why? What in your life now or your past experiences would provide you with the strength to carry on and move forward … no matter what? As you think about this, realize that your thoughts and your strengths are blessings.

Or would you choose to walk away from difficult challenges? Why? What other options would you choose? Realize that the decision to walk away from what you don't feel you can handle is also a blessing.

No matter which path you choose, you are being true to your higher self. Be grateful. Everything is happening exactly as it should.

**We waited and prepared ourselves as much as possible.**

## CHAPTER 13

# To Russia with "Gifts"

*"Giving and receiving are one in the same."*

**— Ram Das**

By the end of November, we had completed all the adoption approval requirements, signed a contract, and were officially placed on the waiting list. We requested two children, an infant girl and a toddler boy.

Ron and I knew that we would have to wait longer for a girl, but we had both grown up with sisters and brothers, and we wanted to have two of each in our family. Courtney had said that she wanted a sister, and Eric wanted a brother. And we thought it would be better for each of our adopted children too.

We provided photographs of ourselves and our children so the adoption agency could "match" facial features and hair color. This helped; even today, I smile as I recall the number of times over the years that people told me, "Elena looks just like you." My reply regarding her birth and adoption was always a conversation starter.

And so we waited and prepared ourselves as much as possible.

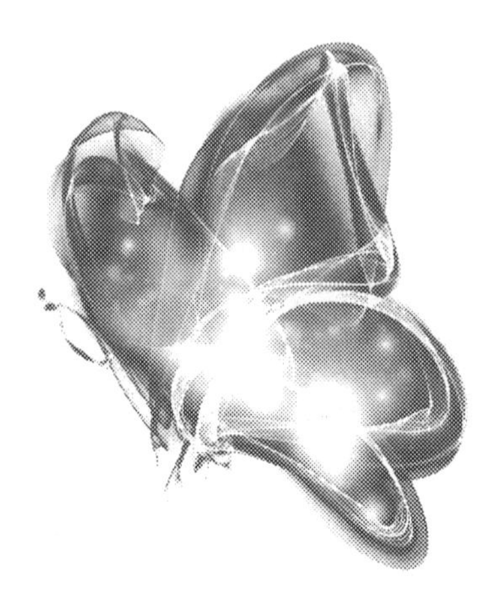

**Elena had big brown curious eyes. Max had a mischievous twinkle in his eyes.**

Shortly after the holidays, in early February 1998, we received two VHS tapes with short videos and a brief medical record for Maxim and Elena, two children at the same orphanage in the region of Astrakhan, located in southern Russia on the banks of the Volga River close to the Caspian Sea.

Elena, then ten months of age, was being held by one of the orphanage caregivers. She had big brown curious eyes, and she managed a little wave and a quick smile. We immediately thought she looked like my sister's son when he was young.

Maxim was holding a doll, prancing around a carpeted room and conversing with the person behind the camera, constantly smiling and continuously on the go. He had a mischievous twinkle in his eyes.

Ninety seconds on each video. That was all. What did we think? Yes! Yes! Yes!

The children's medical records contained phrases about developmental delays, as we had been told expect. Maxim's date of birth indicated he was a mere eighteen months old, which was clearly not right. Judging by his activities on the video, we assumed he was really closer to two-and-a-half and wouldn't find out until closer to our travel date that he was really four—and still a tiny guy—at the time the videos were shot. This news jarred us; thinking he was younger and not yet verbal, Ron and I had not spent much time learning to speak Russian.

Having visually and emotionally accepted these children into our lives, we finally started to call family members to relate the news. I asked Mom to sit down before I told her. Then I asked her and Dad to plan on coming to our house to stay with Courtney and Eric while Ron and I traveled to Russia. Everyone was thrilled and yet nervous for us.

Then we were set in whirlwind motion again. We made plans to travel within the next four to six weeks. Before then, we

**Most Russians were not in favor of international adoption of their children.**

needed visas, vaccinations, gifts and clothing for Maxim and Elena, including winter hats, coats, and boots. We bought infant formula and diapers!

On March 9, we received approval to travel. Our departure would be twelve days later, on March 21. We expedited our visa applications to the Russian consulate. And we booked return flights on the 28th, optimistically hoping that the ten-day waiting period would be waived.

We would fly to Moscow, where we would be met by Marina, our escort, translator, and adoption consultant for the week, and her driver, Uri. There, we would exchange the thousands of dollars that we would carry in cash for rubles. Then we would fly 800 miles south to Astrakhan with a suitcase full of "gifts" for officials, meet Maxim and Elena, fall in love with them (I was sure of that!), convince the social worker and the judge that we would be great parents, get their approval, go back and scoop up the kids, fly back to Moscow, get medical check-ups and passports and travel visas, and come home.

A tall order that sounds more like a covert operation, and in a very real sense, it was. The adoption agency, and later Marina herself, warned us not to advertise the reason of our trip to Russia to anyone—period. On the QT, we were "told"—but not in so many words—that most Russians were not in favor of international adoption of their children because it gave the appearance that they could not take care of their own.

So mum was still the word when we arrived in Moscow on Sunday, March 22, 1998. Marina and Uri were there as planned and took us to the Hotel Ukraina, a five-star luxury hotel in the center of the city, overlooking the Moskva River.

This was ironic because Ron and I had stayed at this very same hotel twelve years earlier. We had been on our honeymoon then, young and adventurous, traveling for three weeks from

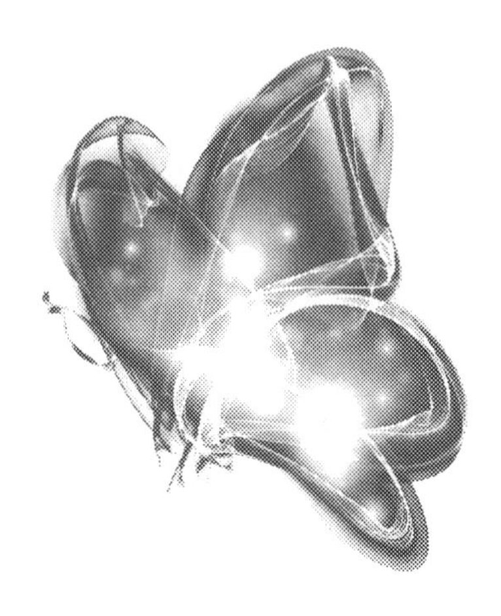

**We were in this together—one more example of our living, breathing wedding vows: "for better or worse" no matter what!**

London through northern Europe, Russia, and Scandinavia. The communist Soviet Union still existed then, and we had traveled the only way possible—with an organized tour.

Much had changed since then, with the dissolution of the Soviet Union in 1991 and the transition to a more capitalistic economy. Yet, I took a great deal of comfort with the time-distanced familiarity of the place. And with Ron's company, of course. We were in this together—one more example of our living, breathing wedding vows: "for better or worse" no matter what!

As soon as we arrived at our hotel room, we pulled out the many hidden plastic bags that we had strapped to our bodies with athletic tape and handed over to Marina the US currency that we had carried into her country.

The amount was $16,000, which would cover the balance of the adoption fees, travel expenses from Moscow to Astrakhan, and medical examinations and visas for Maxim and Elena—all of which would be paid in cash.

What a relief to be rid of the anxiety of carrying that much money! Plus, the plastic had been uncomfortable during our sixteen-hour flight, even with a layer of clothing between the bags and my skin. Of course, this was prior to the bombing of the World Trade Center on September 11, 2001. It would be impossible to carry money out of the US that way today.

Ron and I ventured out of the hotel with our limited to non-existent Russian language skills. We had not bothered to learn the children's mother tongue because we figured they would be too young to speak with us anyway. When we had recently learned that Maxim was four, we had time to only pick up the very basics: *da* (yes), *nyet* (no), *spasibo* (thank you). On the streets of Moscow, we quickly figured out that *pectopah* is the word for restaurant.

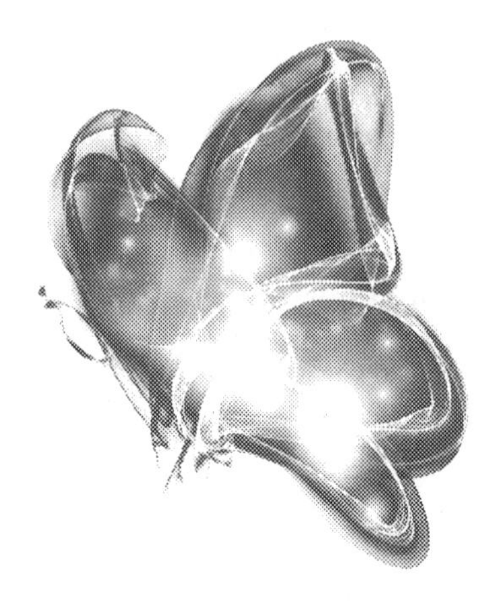

**Both physically and emotionally,
we felt out of place.**

We hopped on the trolley and headed for the Old Arbot Street shopping district in search of Russian treasures to take home as a reminder of where Maxim and Elena came from. We purchased traditional Russian *matryoshka* nesting dolls, porcelain dolls in Russian dress, brightly painted and lacquered wooden boxes, and a wooden stacking-ring toy with an onion dome top.

As we walked the streets, it was very obvious to people we met that we were tourists, foreigners, and clearly not Russian. In addition to our greatly lacking language ability, Ron's bright red ski jacket clearly stood out among the sea of black, brown, gray, and maybe an occasional dark blue coat as well as Russian *ushanka*, large fur hats with ear flaps. Both physically and emotionally, we felt out of place; fortunately, talking about it over a glass of tea in a plaza kiosk helped allay the fears and uncertainty that we both felt.

The next day, on Monday, March 23, we gained some solace when we met our travel companions from Iowa, Susan and her parents David and Ardys. Susan would also be adopting a little girl, Sarah, who was close in age to Elena, from the same orphanage. We spent that day tracking down missing paperwork required by the US embassy and touring the Kremlin and Red Square in the Moscow city center.

The five of us traveled on the Moscow Metro, descending to its subterranean depths on tremendously long escalators that, even at a high speed, take five minutes or more to convey passengers hundreds of feet under the ground to the train tracks below. The beautiful metro stations were lined with marble walls and ceilings decorated with mosaics, chandeliers, and highly detailed bronze sculptures that paid tribute to the Russian *proletariat* of the Communist Era. Walking from one car to another was like traveling through a museum, and there was not one example of graffiti anywhere.

**The Red Square was massive and very impressive but neither red nor square.**

The Red Square was massive and very impressive but neither red in color nor square in shape. The Kremlin had formidable gate houses and tall red brick walls, with its famed merlon-and-crenel battlement from which the fortress gets its name (*kremlin*). One side of the Red Square was the locus of Joseph Lenin's tomb, where that Russian leader's body is preserved within glass for public viewing. Along the other sides of the Red Square were the State History Museum, the GUM State Department Store, and St. Basil's Cathedral with its unique construction of multi-colored and patterned onion shaped domes that is a predominant feature in Russian architecture, particularly in Russian Orthodox churches.

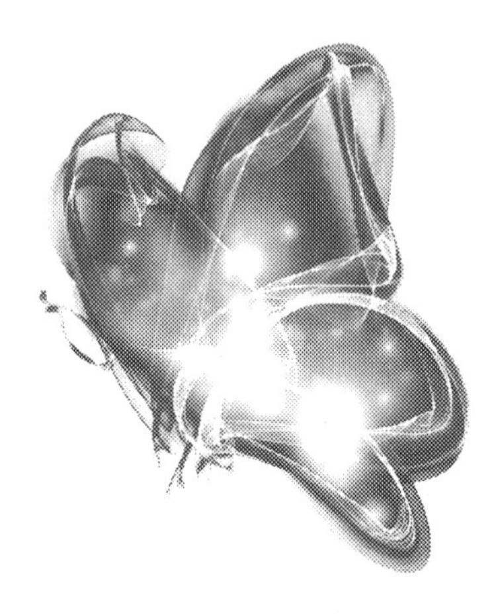

**Everything was so uncertain.**

# CHAPTER 14

# The Great Unknown

*"It is the journey that matters."*

**— Ernest Hemingway**

On Tuesday, Susan, her parents, Ron and I traveled to Astrakhan. The experience was like traveling back in time. The plane we flew on was quite old with fully reclining seats and open overhead luggage racks instead of closed bins. Indeed, the entire plane was antiquated both in its appointments and, we hoped not too much, its mechanics. We breathed another collective sigh of relief when it landed and came to a complete stop on the tarmac.

Our suitcase was full of predetermined "gifts" of vodka, a Seiko watch, and a tape recorder for the adoption officials. We also had clothing, shoes, toy trucks, and dolls that we hoped to give to other children in the orphanage. The suitcases for Susan and her parents were similarly stuffed.

Larissa, a social worker with the title of Minister of Education who would later act as our advocate in front of the judge who would need to approve the adoption, inspected these items to make sure they were "suitable." As I handed them

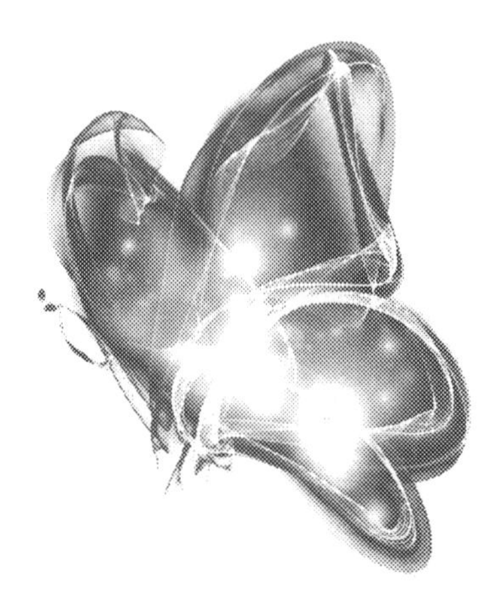

**I felt a tremendous rush of excitement. We had waited so long and done so much. ...Was this really happening?**

over to her, I wondered just how far up the judicial food chain they would travel in order to expedite our request. Everything was so uncertain.

All of us checked into the Lotus Hotel in the center of Astrakhan along the Volga River. The hotel, the largest in the city and built in the early 1970s during the Soviet Era, was quite dated and sparsely decorated with muted wallpaper on the walls, red tapestry carpet, and bright pink tapestry drapes. The bathroom did have a shower, albeit curtain-less; the water supply came through a hose attached to the sink faucet and the drain was simply a hole in the floor. The hotel's dining hall served mashed potatoes and peas for both breakfast and dinner each day we were there.

While the views along the river side could be quite striking, our room at the back of the hotel overlooked the back streets with leafless trees and brown grass. Three older people were sweeping the sidewalk and street with straw brooms and small pans. Watching them in earnest, I wondered, "Is this their way of existence? Is this what Maxim and Elena might grow up doing for work if they don't come home with us?"

After breakfast the next morning, Marina provided "instructions" about what to expect at the orphanage: we would meet the orphanage director in her office and the children would be brought to us; we would have a short time with them; then, assuming we still wanted them—and I knew we would—we would leave them at the orphanage and go to the court to complete the legal part of the adoption. These steps seemed straightforward enough to us, but her manner of delivery made us think that we were part of a subversive operation.

As we headed to the Regional Specialized Orphanage to meet Maxim and Elena, I felt a tremendous rush of excitement. We had waited so long and done so much back in Midland

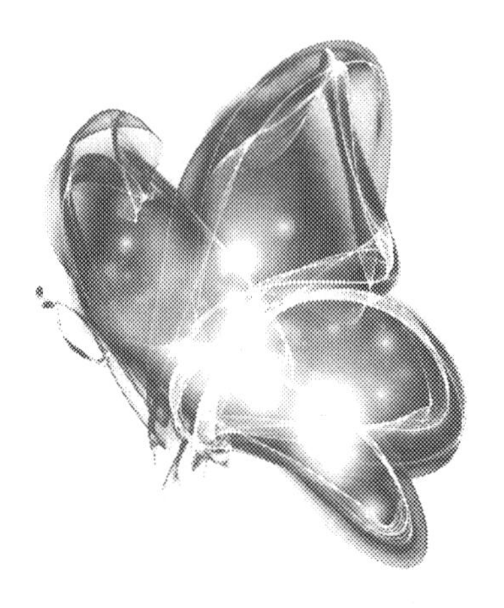

**Was this really happening?**
**Was this form of "birthing" going**
**to become real for us?**

that the duration had seemed unendurable at the time. The flight, with that money taped uncomfortably to our bodies and anxiety churning in our stomachs, seemed to take forever. Now, having arrived in Astrakhan only the night before, the meeting with the children was imminent. I gasped with anticipation and felt the rush of air catch in my throat. Was this really happening? Was this form of "birthing" going to become real for us?

The orphanage was an old, two-story brick building located on a less-traveled side street. It was one of four in Astrakhan, each with a specific purpose. This one was home to approximately 100 orphans from infanthood to age five. Another housed invalid children; another had only children from Astrakhan; and the last was for school-age children over five and is where Maxim would have moved to in the coming year.

Inside the gate, we passed a small fenced-in playground area with a few rusty swings that gave the impression it was not regularly used. A strong smell of bleach greeted us inside the orphanage door. The muted colors on the walls indicated that an application of fresh paint, or even a good scrubbing, was a rare occurrence, although some child-oriented decorations did indicate a feeble attempt to bring a feeling of "home" to the poorly-lit interior.

Having met the director, we waited for the children: Maxim, Elena, and Sarah. Soon came the sound of a young boy crying in the hallway. Maxim? Through the doorway, I saw someone give a piece of candy to the child, and then he walked confidently into the office, smiling. I loved him at first sight! But, later, I would recall that moment. Was that an early indication that Maxim, at four years and three months of age, had already learned how to "play the system?" When we showed the stuffed toys that Courtney and Eric had picked out for Elena and Maxim, he quickly grabbed them and hung on to them tightly.

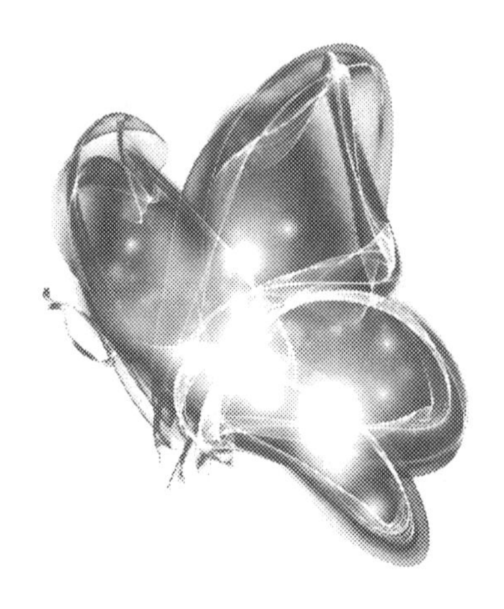

**Both children were social orphans. . . .
And I knew only too well that
I wasn't going to leave these
two here forever!**

The three children wore nice clothing that someone had slipped over the top of their regular clothing. We quickly determined that these were "show clothes," donated by a previous adoption family and rotated as necessary when children were shown to prospective adoptive parents. The double-layer of clothing made them look heavier than they actually were.

Ron and I were given forty-five minutes to get acquainted with the children, which was easy enough with Elena, because of her age, but a challenge with Maxim because he wanted to talk and we didn't share a common language. Marina helped by introducing us as "Momma and Poppa."

We sat on the floor with both kids, watching and talking to them as best we could while they looked at us and the social worker observed all.

Ron's beard was a curiosity to both children, who rarely saw men at the orphanage. Maxim was very social and entertaining while Elena was quiet, looking as if she had never seen so many people at one time. Maybe she never had. Just how different was this interaction with us from her life in a crib?

Both children were social orphans. Elena's mother was not married and worked as a shop clerk in the area. Her father was a restaurant waiter. Maxim's parents were married and his father was described as deaf and mute from a childhood illness. Maxim had entered the orphanage more than two years earlier at two years, one month.

As a mom in the US, I tried not to think what his life has been like during so many of his critical formative years. And how would all of that play out at home in the States?

Our visit was short and we were too-soon told that it was time for us to leave Maxim and Elena at the orphanage. I didn't want to leave, yet I knew we must. We had the "official

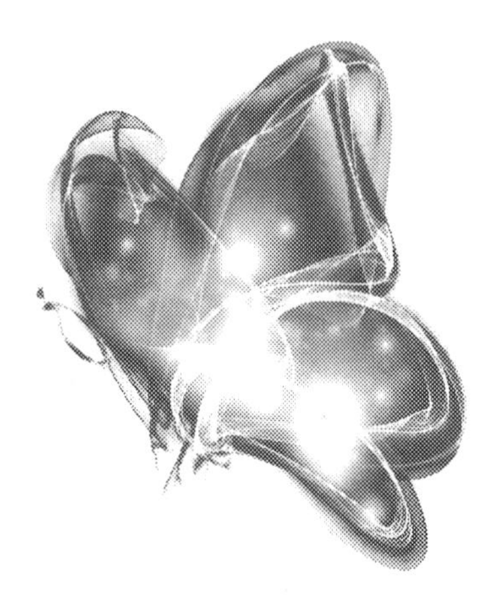

**Did you ever have to make up your mind?**

business" of adoption to take care of if we were to fulfill the purpose of our mission here. And I knew only too well that I wasn't going to leave these two here forever! So, yes, I would forsake my heart for a few more hours as we applied our minds to the tasks at hand.

Walking out, I wondered how Maxim's mom could have abandoned him. But did she? More likely, she and her husband had made the necessary, hard, but caring and compassionate sacrifice that would enable her son to have a better life with others … whomever they might be … wherever they might live.

**TIME OUT**

Did you ever have to make up your mind about something really, really big and important … something more significant than what car to buy or what color you want to paint a room?

The hardest decisions are those of life and death: to birth or abort, to sustain life support or to let go and await a loved one's last breath. To give up for adoption or not. Maybe you've been in a place of making the necessary, hard, but caring decisions. Imagine yourself in one of these decision places, or in the position of Maxim's or Elena's mother and father in Russia. Knowing that your decisions become your story, what would you decide to do? How do you find peace in your decision process?

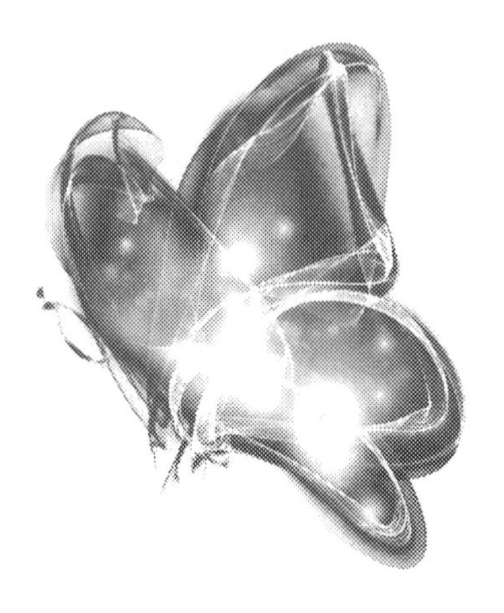

**How much extra care?**
**What are we getting ourselves in for?**

# CHAPTER 15

## The System

*"Government's first duty is to protect the people."*

**— Ronald Reagan**

As we entered the government building where we were to complete the adoption, we saw that Larissa, who would present our request, was already there. Marina, our translator, told us to watch her while the judge asked questions; she said she would motion with her hand when to answer "da" and nod our heads.

After many minutes, Ron and I, along with Marina and Larissa, were called into the judge's chambers. Susan remained seated in the antechamber, awaiting her turn.

The judge's office was small, with a subtle dank odor and one small corner window. He sat at a small corner desk, the epitome of stoicism, as we stood before him.

He asked why we wanted to adopt, why we wanted to adopt children from Russia, where we live and work, whether our other children know Maxim and Elena would be adopted from Russia, and if we knew they will need extra care.

The questions about us and Eric and Courtney were easy to answer; the question about "extra care" was tougher. *How*

**We felt that the Russian system wanted to make sure their adopted children went to good homes**

*much extra care? What are we getting ourselves in for?* Yet, we—Ron especially—answered "da" with ease as I pushed aside thoughts about Stephanie. I had given birth to her not knowing what we were truly in for. Certainly, bringing home two healthy children from Russia can't be any worse.

Can it?

Larissa told the judge that she supported the adoption, saying that we had met the children and they liked us. She asked the judge to waive the ten-day waiting period because we needed to return to our other children and we were anxious to be together as an entire family.

This was a tense moment because if he said "*nyet,*" we would have to change our return flight, and I didn't want this process to continue a moment longer than necessary. After many exchanges and nodding of heads, the judge honored her request and approved the adoption. The date was March 25, 1998, and the children, according to the decree of a Russian judge, were soon to be officially in our care.

We spent the rest of the day driving to multiple government buildings to obtain birth certificates, adoption certificates, and passports. We were given Maxim's baptismal certificate from the Russian Orthodox Church. So much paperwork to complete.

We were nearly exhausted with running hither and yon when Marina took us back to our hotel. We collapsed on the bed and lay staring at the ceiling in our well-worn smelly clothes. Ron spoke of his opinion of this multi-layered process. I nearly cried with laughter when Ron joked that this "red tape" was emanating from people who the US, during the Cold War, referred to as "the Reds."

Then he became more serious. Considering the great joy the adoption would bring to our entire family, the process, with all its paperwork, was a necessary evil. Early on, like when we first saw the VHS tapes that the adoption agency had sent to

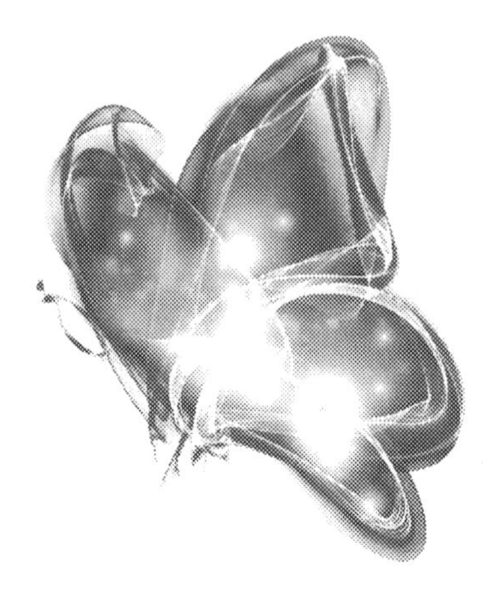

**Can you . . . see the greater good that lies beyond the challenge?**

us, we felt like we were shopping for children. Here, we felt that the Russian system wanted to make sure their adopted children went to good homes—albeit at a price.

Yet, it was clear that many officials benefited financially from the process and not much of the fees, which totaled more than $20,000, would end up at the orphanage where the children had limited food and not enough caretakers. Philosophically, we acquiesced that all of the "gifts"—a bottle of vodka for the judge, a nice Seiko watch for the social worker, and others—was necessary to achieve our goal. "None of these things matter compared to the gifts we can give to Maxim and Elena, our children," we agreed.

I set my personal cares aside and fell asleep wondering how and what Maxim and Elena were doing in their last night in the orphanage. And how different tomorrow night would be for them and for us.

Oh, please, God, make tomorrow night—and every night—be different. Different and better. Infinitely better.

**TIME OUT**

Think of all the people who Linda and Ron encountered on this journey, all of the people who were part of the Russian adoption system. Think of their roles. Consider their purpose. Do you see "who they were" in the process? Do you see "what they were there for"?

Now think of other people you have encountered in your life, either internationally or domestically, who you feel might have challenged you in some way, people you feel put their job or "the system" ahead of your needs and desires.

How do you feel at those moments? Do you feel angry or frustrated? Or do you look upon these individuals still as people who are trying to do their job, fulfilling their roles? Can you accept the outcome of their information and rise above the situation, seeing the greater good that lies beyond the challenge?

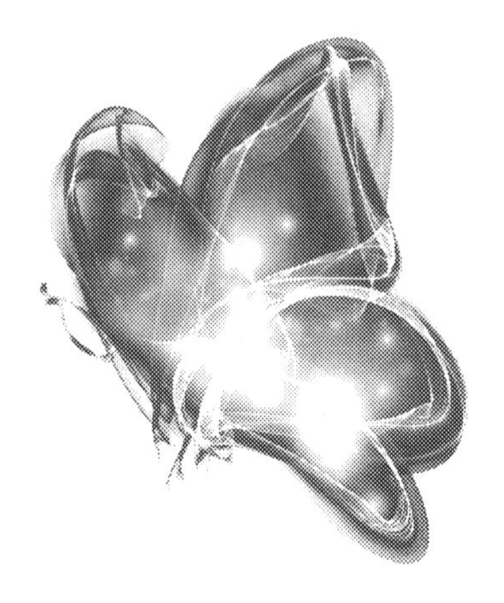

**Life goes on.**

## CHAPTER 16

# The Final Perspective

*"Belief is powerful indeed."*

**— A Course in Miracles**

The next morning, we had some time to walk the streets of Astrakhan before picking up Maxim and Elena—our soon-to-be new children. In that short time, we caught a glimpse and created an impression of this city beyond what we had seen at the airport, hotel, orphanage, and judge's office.

Astrakhan is a city of a half million people. It occupies both sides of the Volga. And although situated in a region with vast natural resources, the city did not appear to be prosperous.

Yet, I had the sensation it had previously been a more beautiful place. Many of the once-magnificent brick buildings were in a state of decay with crumbling bricks, chipped paint, and faded colors. The streets were lined with cars that looked twenty years old; some of them might not have been started or moved in weeks, and I wondered if they even had petrol in their tanks, or if the owners could afford to buy any.

The feeling of dreariness or long-lost prosperity was intensified by heavy overcast clouds and the few number of people on

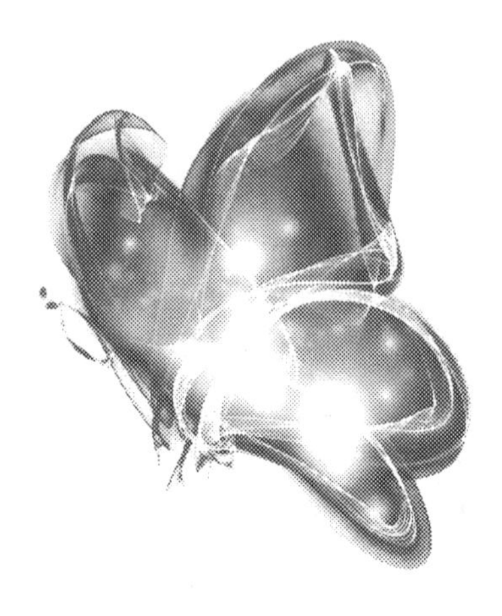

**Oh, God, please help our two new Russian children not find their new home to be too different**

the streets, except for several gypsy children begging for a handout. Cold winds off the Caspian Sea chilled the air while remnants of an overnight snowfall lingered. Still, a vendor set up his stand on a street corner, hoping to sell fresh fruit.

Looking down an alley, I saw laundry hung out to dry, a sign that life goes on. At that moment, for some strange reason, my mind flashed back to our home in Midland and I wondered aloud to Ron about how our Eric and Courtney might be doing. "Do you suppose they're doing the laundry?" I asked, and he, with his ever-present kindness, assured me they were.

We walked by a white-washed hospital building that was only distinguishable by an army green ambulance reminiscent of something seen in the *M*A*S*H* television series.

The visual highlight of the Astrakhan landscape was another *kremlin* battlement wall that marked a former city fortress now converted to a museum.

On one corner stood the green-and gold-domed Russian Orthodox Assumption Cathedral. The five domes symbolized Christ and the four evangelists: Matthew, Mark, Luke, and John—Christian symbols in a nation that our nation once deemed agnostic.

Outside the *kremlin* walls, in Lenina Square, stood a prominent statue of Lenin. The square was tidy with snow removal performed by ordinary-looking citizens with snow shovels. Except for the name on the figure, the scene could have been Central Park in New York City.

Last night, I had prayed that the days and nights in Midland would be vastly different for Maxim and Elena than the days and nights they had experienced in the orphanage. Today, I edited my thoughts: *Oh, God, please help our two new Russian children not find their new home to be too different—at least in their young minds—from their native homeland.*

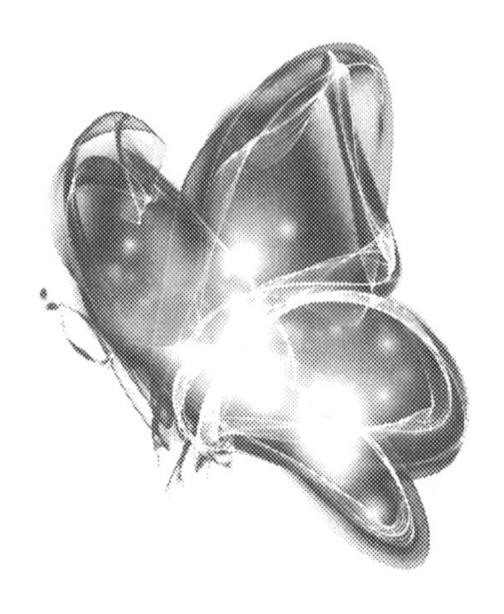

**Maxim again entertained everyone in the room with his effervescent chatter.**

We arrived at the orphanage after lunch with clothing for Maxim and Elena and a photo book to show Maxim his soon-to-be new home, family, and pets. He called us Momma and Poppa again when he arrived at the director's office, and I wondered if he had been practicing through the night. *Had he been coached?*

Our new kids were accompanied by a string of caregivers, likely curious to catch a glimpse of the latest adoptive families. Elena's caregiver insisted on undressing her one more time, peeling back the layers of "show clothes" and her flannel jump suit and thus revealing that she was a skinny, fifteen-pound, but beautiful little girl. While not yet old enough to walk, Elena stood by herself for a few seconds for her public disrobing. She was teething and content to suck on three fingers at once.

Maxim again entertained everyone in the room with his effervescent chatter. At less than twenty-five pounds, he, too, was smaller than we imagined—or should have been for a child of his age. The shoes we had brought from home were several sizes too large for his tiny feet.

We dressed the children—our children—in clothes we had brought from the United States, and they left the orphanage without a single possession from their life in Russia. *I hope they're too young to notice.*

While Susan finished her paperwork to adopt Sarah, Ron and I were offered the chance to tour the orphanage, not a common practice. We jumped at the opportunity with camera in hand. We were shown Elena's communal nursery room, Maxim's communal bedroom, a medical treatment room, and several small play rooms that contained a few toys, small tables and chairs, and a small TV with rabbit ears.

One room was recognizable from the video we had previously received that showed Maxim talking and playing with other

**The caregivers loved the children and provided the best care they could, albeit with limited resources.**

boys. Elena's nursery room contained a dozen cribs under the care of one worker, which meant there was minimal individual human interaction for each child on a daily basis.

It was obvious that the caregivers loved the children and provided the best care they could, albeit with limited resources and the large number of children they were responsible for. But, as a mom who had birthed and nursed two healthy children—and a third I had so little opportunity to hold—my heart went out to both the workers and the children there.

As we peeked into Maxim's room, the boys with whom he had shared that room were settling in for a nap with their heads sticking out from under a dark gray, woolen blanket. They cast their eyes as if to ask, "Are you here for me?" My heart yearned to speak, *Oh, I would love to be here for you and take you home with me.* But my mind prevailed: two—or four, counting Courtney and Eric—were enough.

At the same time, the mom in me was pleased to see that the orphanage was very clean and all the children followed a strict daily schedule of sleeping, eating, hygiene, and play time. For the older children, there was scheduled time in the various play rooms. For the infants, it appeared they were placed in four-foot-square, elevated, covered wooden boxes with four cutouts for their arms and legs, where they could be placed and sit facing each other.

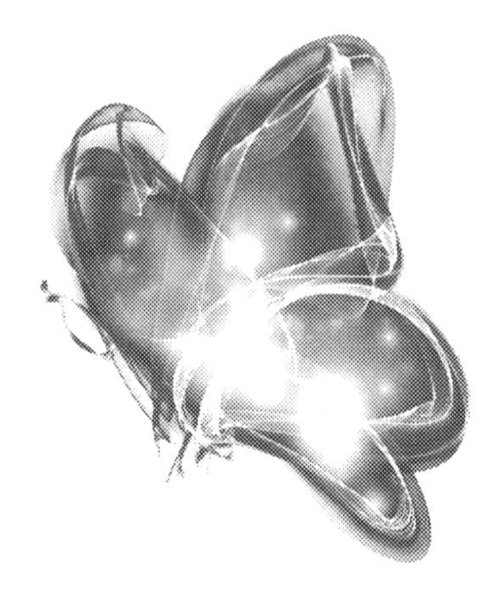

**Change is the only constant.**

## CHAPTER 17

# From Russia, With Love

*"Adoption: When your family tree becomes an orchard."*

**— unknown**

Before we left, the orphanage director and several of the caregivers posed for photos with Maxim and Elena. Their half smiles and tears told me that they were sad to see them leave. I took this, as well as the fact that they carried Maxim and Elena outside to the car before handing them over to us, as a sign of love and appreciation for these two darling children. I knew I would be loving too, yet my hand and heart trembled a bit as I refused to think about what challenges the next several years would bring for all of us.

Change is the only constant, I reminded myself.

As we drove to the airport, Maxim was fascinated by all the cars and trucks on the roads; he frequently said, "Beep-beep," and called out, "*mah-SHI-nah.*"

We flew back to Moscow on another antiquated airplane, with both kids sitting on our laps, not constrained by seatbelts.

Maxim was very hungry and ate continuously, stuffing food in his mouth with one hand while stashing what he could under

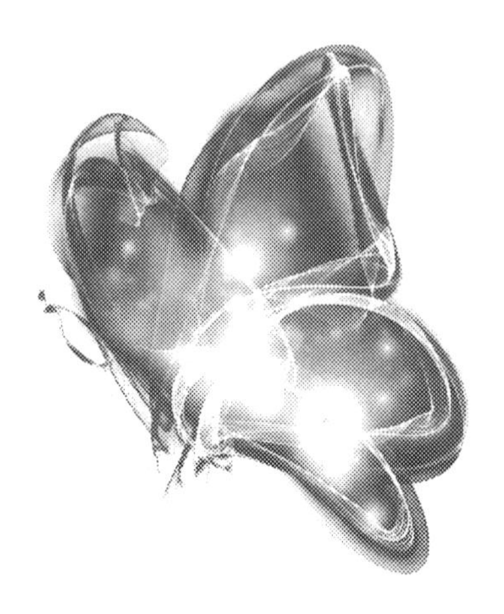

# Maxim: somewhat of an "unusual child."

his arm; we would later surmise this was a technique learned at the orphanage to secretly hide a between-meal snack. He was also very active and talked non-stop to anyone and everyone on the plane. We, of course, didn't know much of what he was saying, but we were clued in enough to know he was coming to realize he had "flown the coop" and his days at the orphanage were, as Ernie Harwell often said of homeruns, "loooong gone!"

Once back in Moscow, we were re-joined by Uri, our driver, who spoke to Maxim in Russian and later, at the hotel, got him to sit calmly in his lap. Their conversations and laughter were endless, but we knew nothing of what they said.

The paperwork process continued with visa applications for both children, medical examinations, and translation of the birth certificates, adoption documents, and medical records that the orphanage had provided.

Maxim's early medical history was missing, so we learned only that he had entered the orphanage at two years and one month of age after spending the required six-months restriction in a hospital, that he had weighed less than fifteen pounds then, and that he did not start walking until two months later.

The doctor estimated his physical development to be delayed by one-and-a-half years, but he was otherwise healthy and surprisingly outgoing. Normally, the doctor told us, children who are institutionalized for several years are very withdrawn and unattached, so he looked upon Maxim as somewhat of an "unusual child" … a prophetic diagnosis!

Finally, after jumping through so many governmental and bureaucratic hoops in only a few days, we were alone in the hotel room with our new children. That night, they got their first taste of pizza, a delight for both, and we had our first opportunity to reflect on what life in the orphanage might have been like for them.

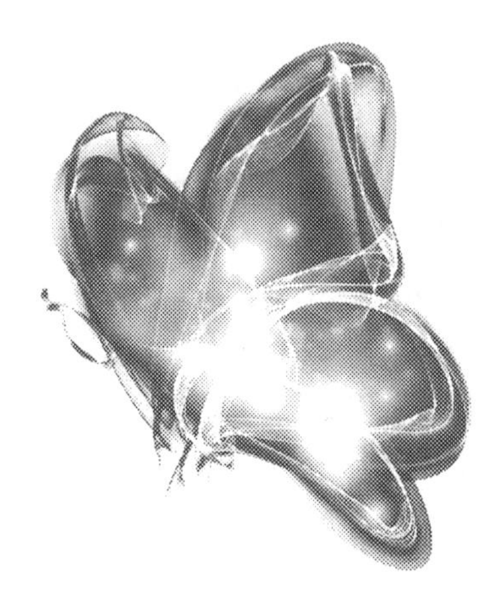

**With soft hearts and tears forming in our eyes, we picked them up and held them until they fell asleep in our arms.**

By observing their weight and actions, it was easy to imagine that the amount and nutritional value of the food was probably limited. For many years afterward, Maxim would eat food with one hand while holding more food with the other, and he was also compelled to sneak food away from the dinner table to eat it later even though he could have asked for and received whatever he wanted at any time.

When we placed Elena on the carpet with several toys to play with, she just sat there, not making a peep, not moving, acting as if she were still confined by her crib or the "play box." We wondered if she could actually make a sound but soon rationalized that crying in a room with ten other infants and one caregiver wouldn't result in any immediate attention, so the children probably learned in their unique childlike way, "Why bother?" We also accurately predicted that this quietness would go away once she got home and realized how to get her older sister's immediate attention, which she did by making little sounds that Courtney could not resist.

Neither Maxim nor Elena liked to take a bath or shower, which indicated that that must have not been a pleasant experience in the orphanage.

When we put both kids to bed that first night, they both immediately, as if on cue, put three fingers into their mouths and started to rock themselves back and forth to fall asleep, another characteristic of institutionalism that they would retain for many years. With soft hearts, and tears forming in my eyes, we picked them up and held them until they fell asleep in our arms. No doubt, a first for them.

We spent Friday, our last day in Moscow, at the US Embassy being interviewed by the consulate and getting visas approved for Maxim and Elena. Ron also took Maxim on a shopping trip

**I began to appreciate his inherent curiosity. . . . I began to shake with exhaustion and relief.**

for a pair of shoes that actually fit his feet as well as a few souvenirs from their homeland.

On Saturday, March 28, 1998, we flew home, happy to be on Aeroflot Airlines with flight attendants who spoke Russian and helped him be calm and remain buckled in his seat. The nine-hour flight to Chicago was long with both kids not sleeping well and Maxim having an upset stomach and constant trips to the bathroom, probably due to all the new, rich foods he was eating.

We had a four-hour layover at Chicago's O'Hare airport where Maxim tasted his first McDonald's French fries and spent the entire time looking out a concourse window, mesmerized by the airport ground traffic. I began to appreciate his inherent curiosity, which he would further reveal in many, many ways.

We finally arrived home in Midland late that night, after more than 20 hours of travel from our hotel in Moscow. Disembarking from the airplane, we each carried one child and seemed to be the main attraction among the passengers and other travelers in the concourse.

Finally, in the baggage claim area, we were met by family and more than a dozen friends who shared laughter and tears of joy as they passed the children around from one to another. My dad used his handkerchief to wipe tears from his eyes, the one and only time Ron had ever seen him cry. My heart leapt as I realized that he had already accepted Elena and Maxim as his new grandchildren.

At that moment, standing there, I began to shake with exhaustion and relief. Six months and two weeks after our first meeting with an adoption agent, we were now, officially, a family of six. Or seven, if you include Stephanie who, I'm sure, is still with us in some mysterious, wonderful, saintly way … even if only in my mind.

**See the process filled with love, desire, and sacrifice.**

**TIME OUT**

Most of us know someone in an adoption circumstance. Recall them—or, if adoption is a part of your life story—see the process filled with love, desire, and sacrifice, as defined in *Sportuality* as being "to make holy." This adoption was holy, or "whole," in that it was a physical, mental, emotional and indeed, spiritual. Take a moment to recall the gratitude you feel for all the adopted children in your life.

# THE POWER OF QUESTION

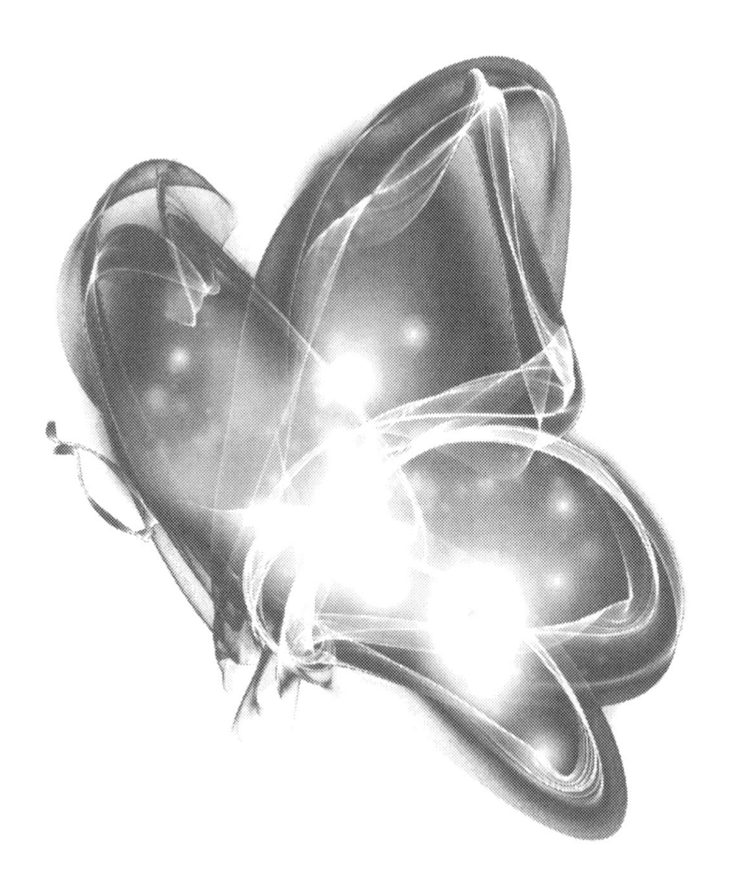

# THE POWER OF QUESTION

Socrates created the Socratic Method to teach by questioning. Jesus said, "Ask and you shall receive." Einstein implored, "Question everything."

These great teachers and way showers are reminding us of what we innately know … that we grow by questioning, by participating in a meeting of the minds, by creating an exchange of ideas. This is affirmed by any life coach or motivational teacher who tells us that questions are the way to engage others in a higher level of thinking.

With a 35-year college volleyball coaching career in my rear-view mirror, it was this year that three critical questions, following a loss by my team, came across my screen:

"What went well during this game?"

"What do we need to work on?"

"In what ways are we better because we lost today?"

I've always tried to find ways to help my teams deal with loss and disappointment, and these three questions were helpful in encouraging us to reflect and to move forward. Isn't that what we need to do on a daily basis? Move forward, ever forward.

Now Max, when he was a seventh-grade student, may not have understood the Socratic Method or known of the work of Einstein, but Max has always had a rich Christian faith. He knew to ask in order to receive. So he turned and interjected those existential questions—"Who are you?" "What are you here for?"—into my path as he and I began our fledgling relationship.

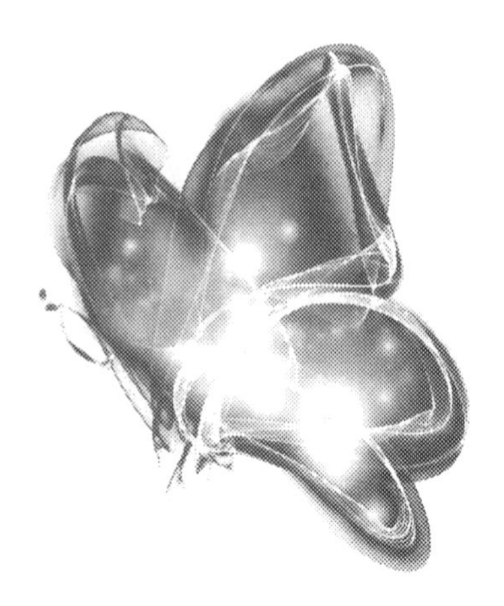

**Elena and Maxim weren't blank slates. … What thoughts might have been running through their young minds?**

# CHAPTER 18

## The Lion

*"You weren't just adopting us, but our pasts as well."*

**— Saroo Brierly, in *Lion***

In a very touching scene in the movie *Lion,* adopted child Saroo Brierly, then a grown man (played by Dev Patel), says to his adoptive mother, Sue Brierly (played by Nicole Kidman), "I mean, we [me and my adopted brother] weren't like blank pages, were we? Like your own would have been. You weren't just adopting us, but our pasts as well."

Linda and Ron could see from the outset that Elena and Maxim weren't blank slates. These children came to their parents with lots of inscriptions written in their development years: Elena was cautiously reserved, and Maxim was outgoing and curious. Both had special needs—naturally, considering that they were "social orphans," abandoned by birth parents and accepted by receptive parents who they met for a few minutes in the orphanage director's office.

What thoughts might have been running through their young minds on that day? Did they know enough at their young ages, from watching other children mysteriously disappear, that that day might also represent their day to leave the orphanage?

What realizations came to them that same night in the hotel room in Astrakhan, during the airplane ride to Moscow, while in the hotel and scurrying around in Moscow, and, perhaps most of all, as they traveled

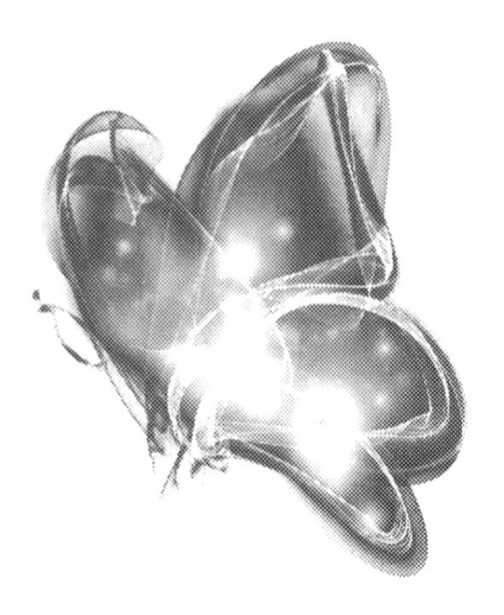

**The unknowing can be terrible and problematic.**

that long, 20-hour plane trip to Chicago and then Midland, Michigan, a city that by its very name seems to epitomize America's stereotypical "Midwest"?

At what point (or points) does a child's mind transition feelings of being uprooted to thoughts of being accepted? How and when does an orphan child's brain process the multiple associations of being with birth mother, then hospital nurse, then orphanage caregiver, then adoptive parents? Do they even comprehend the word "adoptive?" When does a child, further matured and cognitive, begin to appreciate and be grateful for the efforts of all of these people as well as the governmental legal systems that make adoption—international or domestic—possible?

At what age or stage of development does any child—adopted or not—begin to ask of themselves, "Who am I? What am I here for?" and to ask of others, "Who are *these* people? What are *they* here, in my life, for?"

In *Lion*, Saroo Brierly, who was born in India and raised by the Brierlys in Australia, acknowledges that he thought about his birth mother every day. Knowing that he had become lost by inadvertently falling asleep on a train that, overnight, traveled hundreds of kilometers from his home, young Saroo knows that his mother has no idea of where he is. Might she think he's been killed or swept away by a hurricane or plucked off the streets by human traffickers?

The unknowing can be terrible and problematic, as it was for Saroo.

**TIME OUT**

Think about cultural differences and racial/ethnic differences. Think about what it would be like—or has been like—for you to bring someone who is "different" in some way into your home, your family, your life.

Think about how the questions "Who am I? Who are you?" and "What am I here for?" and "What are you here for?" resonate—or resonate differently—for an adopted child or an abandoned street child than for a child raised by birthparents. Would such a child even consciously think of such questions?

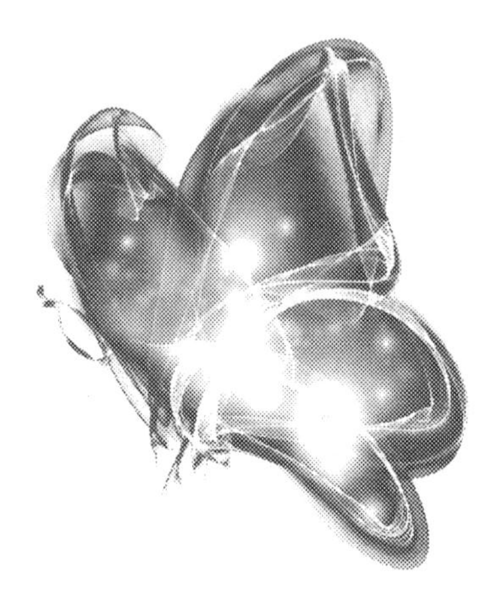

**Education is really a self-exploration.**

# CHAPTER 19

# Education

*"Every step forward is a step toward achieving something bigger."*

**— Brian Tracy**

In the American culture—and probably the cultures of many nations—the word "education" has taken on a passive meaning. Teachers and parents "educate" while children "receive an education."

*Sportuality*, however, reminds readers of the original intent of the word "education"—to draw forth, to bring out the best in others and the best in ourselves. Education, then, is really a self-exploration and self-examination of what we have within our internal selves and what we can observe and learn from our external surroundings and the people around us.

Max's education consisted of several formal steps as well as unique experiences: the orphanage, certainly; his adoptive home and family life with the Nartkers; the Midland Public Schools; nearby Delta Community College; an internship with WCEN Radio, an FM country-and-western station near Midland that refers to itself as "The Moose;" meeting and interacting in the broadcast booths with Detroit Tigers television announcers Rod Allen and Mario Impemba and Tigers radio announcers Jim Price and Dan Dickerson; and viewing Mitch Albom's stage play *Ernie*, which touched him immensely.

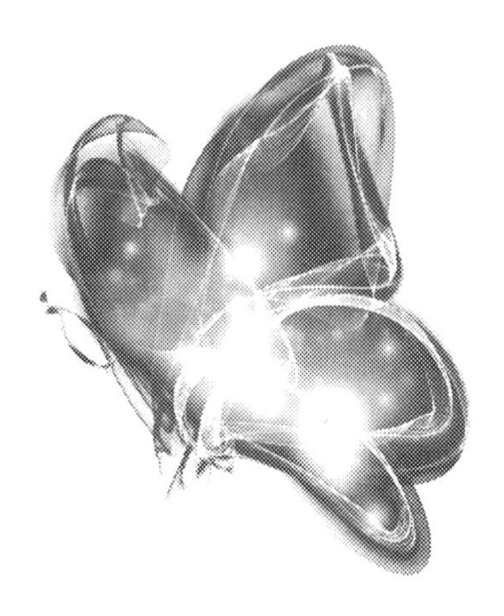

**"Nothing great was ever achieved without enthusiasm!"**

One of the highlights of Max's education occurred at the graduation of his senior class when he, an adopted citizen, delivered the commencement address to his classmates, where he referenced the Chemics, a school mascot so named because of the influence of the Dow Chemical Company, Midland's largest employer. He said:

> I am so excited that the graduation committee asked me to speak to you about what it means to be a Chemic. Here's what I think makes us Chemics!
>
> Chemics are enthusiastic!
>
> One thing I like about Midland High is that we are LOUD and PROUD! School assemblies, the band marching in the hallways, and the student sections during football and basketball games are memories I will always keep because they represent our Chemic pride and our Class. As Ralph Waldo Emerson once said, "Nothing great was ever achieved without enthusiasm!"
>
> Chemics are really involved!
>
> I've really enjoyed my time here at MHS because there was always something to do and ways for me to be involved. From sports teams and music groups to photography and Key Club, there is an activity for everyone.
>
> Chemics are helpful and generous!
>
> Another way we show Chemic pride is by being helpful to other people. The amount of help doesn't even have to be that much. It could be something really small, like one day between second and third hour I dropped my folder and someone stopped to help me get my papers back into it. Or it could be something big, like when our Student Council organizes a fundraiser for Kids Against Hunger.
>
> Chemics are positive and care about each other!

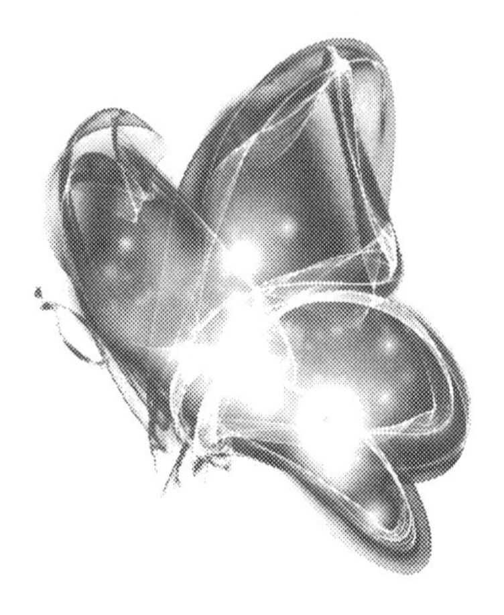

**Each of us brings a gift to this party called life.**

Probably one thing I like best about Midland High is that there are so many nice people who care about you and want you to succeed in life. Like Mrs. Greif, who is going to outlive us all. She's always positive and concerned about everyone's well-being. I think that is also a big part of Chemic pride.

We are so lucky there are a lot of really helpful people here at MHS, and as Chemics, this isn't going to stop just because we aren't in high school anymore.

A wise woman once told me that we are only a phone call, text message, tweet or Facebook message away. So remember that!

Also be sure to thank the people who have helped you, especially your families, for all their support and dedication the last four years.

So to me, Chemics are Enthusiastic! Helpful! Generous! Positive! And Kind!

All of which makes Chemic Pride: a very special tradition!

Thank you!

Max is an educator to all: his classmates, their family and friends, me, and now you, as you read this. Why? Because, with his searing curiosity and outgoing nature, he inspires us to draw forth our inner selves.

You are also an educator to all, for the same reason. Each of us brings a gift to this party called life. Each of us has a responsibility and an opportunity to get up off our gifts and inspire others to draw forth their inner talents and gifts.

The education I draw forth from Max's speech is filled with gratitude, enthusiasm (he uses lots of exclamation points), compliments, humor, and personal experiences. His message is inclusive, kind, caring and compassionate. His words are concise and well-crafted, which is good because a broadcaster—an Ernie Harwell—must hold audience interest.

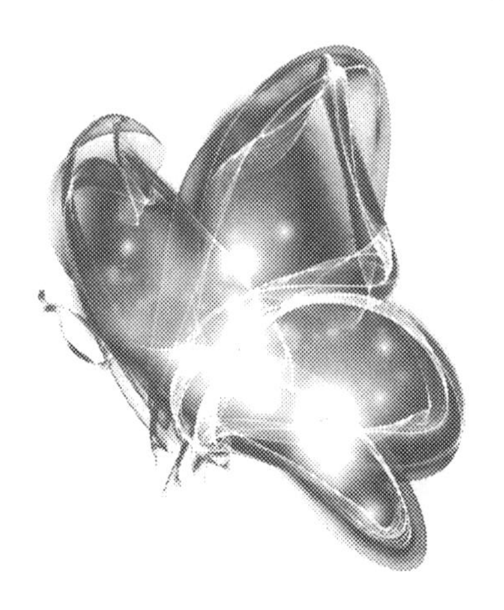

**He unites with his emotion, through his intelligence, and by inviting them into his spiritual reality.**

For credibility, he includes the name of a famous person, Ralph Waldo Emerson. He also mentions the Chemics name often, a branding technique. He speaks the names of teachers who bonded with the students, a sign that he knows his audience. And Max invites his classmates to remain in supportive contact with each other as members of the same school community.

He unites with his emotion, through his intelligence, and by inviting them into his spiritual reality.

He reminds them repeatedly of who they are: Chemics. And what they are here in high school for: To be proud of who they are … among other things.

**TIME OUT**

Education is a lifelong process. Whatever your educational status, whether you are formally in school, receiving on-the-job training, or experiencing life in your own way, what are you doing at this point in your life to draw forth your greater, higher self? What are you doing to become "your Ernie"? What questions have been most helpful in your growth?

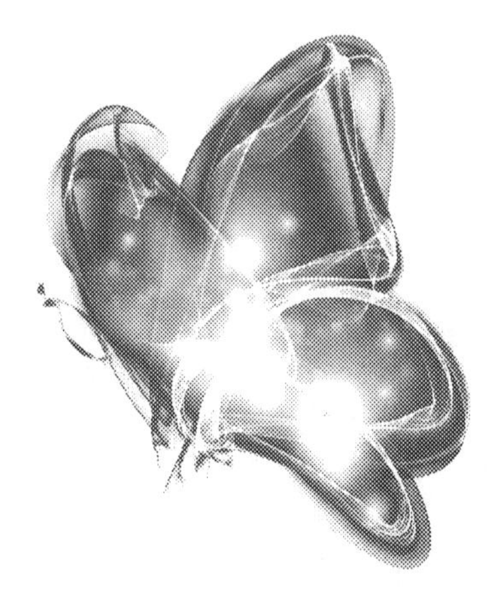

**Just like each one of us,**
**Max also faces challenges.**

## CHAPTER 20

# Becoming Ernie

*"You can do anything you set your mind to."*

**— Benjamin Franklin**

As I mentioned earlier, Ernie Harwell had to overcome a speech impediment before he could be accepted as even a rookie broadcaster. And he worked hard to do that. Just like each one of us, Max also faces challenges. Those challenges are educational opportunities for him—as our challenges are for us.

Throughout his childhood and into early adulthood, Max's challenges included attention-deficit/hyperactive disorder (ADHD). He has a hard time sitting still, which can be a big problem for a broadcaster who has to sit behind a microphone for an entire game.

Max speaks without filters. He says what he wants whenever he wants. He's usually humorous if not downright funny, but sometimes his audience is put off by his brashness.

Personally, I find Max to be refreshing. Plus, I'm grateful. If not for Max's bold mannerisms, he would not have blasted me with the foundational questions that are the theme for this book ... and for life.

Interestingly, Max and his dynamic personality also brought forward a creative solution to a problem that faced Joby Phillips, the afternoon

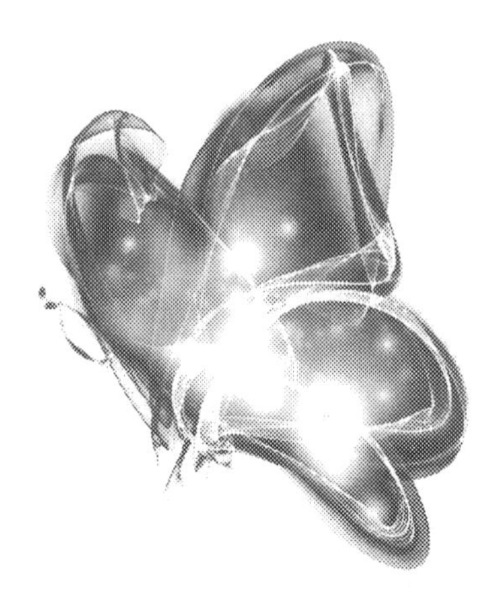

**"Last night, I dreamt that I was a muffler, and I woke up exhausted!"**

disk jockey at WCEN in Saginaw, Michigan. Phillips explained that Max was one of four people who applied for an internship at The Moose, but he was the only one who returned phone calls. "He was persistent, and he was really serious about wanting the position," Phillips said. "Passionate," was another word he used to describe Max; from my previous experiences with Max, I would use the word "enthusiastic." Sometimes "over-the-top enthusiastic."

Phillips recalled that Max's first day as being fun, humorous, and, in his words, "a riot." But while Max was quick-witted, honest, and open—due to not being hindered by "social filters"—he was also easily distracted, a characteristic of attention deficit disorder.

Being a supervisor at the station, Phillips knew that he had a responsibility to draw the best possible performance out of Max. How to accomplish that? ADHD and radio don't necessarily make good bedfellows. He coached Max regarding the details of creating a radio show, with all its playlists, rotations, research, and focus. But how to get Max on the air? This was among the questions that Joby asked himself.

One day while driving to work, Phillips heard a radio personality known as Surfer Dude enter another announcer's program with a short, sweet, humorous observation about life. "Max can do that!" he exclaimed. So he told Max to come up with a bunch of corny jokes—short one-liners.

With this new assignment in mind, Max contacted my husband, who is a master of the corny joke, asking for ideas. Imagine my delight when, one day, an email from Max came with an attached audio file. It began with DJ Joby Phillips' voice, choreographically interrupted by Max, saying: "Hey, Joby. Last night, I dreamt that I was a muffler, and I woke up exhausted!"

Phillips believes that Max's talent lies not behind a microphone—sharp-witted and full of data as his mind is—but as a writer. He was impressed by a eulogy Max delivered as well as the ten-page paper he wrote about his internship on which he received an "A" grade.

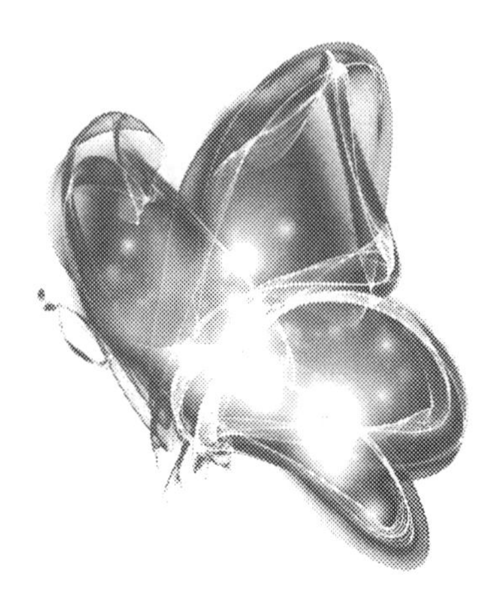

**Essentially, we are all each other's educators. We simply need to ask the questions!**

While Joby would most likely not consider himself an educator, his role in Max's life at this moment was pivotal in drawing forth Max's gifts. Essentially, we are all each other's educators. We simply need to ask the questions!

Whether or not Max Nartker becomes a professional sports announcer is irrelevant, even though he had declared his intent to walk in the footsteps of the great Ernie Harwell. Then, much to his consternation, in his last semester prior to graduation, Delta College cancelled their broadcast education curriculum.

What did Max do? On the Earthly horizontal plane, he fussed for a while, then he went forward and got a job in the kitchen at a famous restaurant in nearby Frankenmuth, Michigan. On the vertical spiritual axis, he went inside and asked himself: Who am I *now?* What am I here for *now?*

He drew forth this great spiritual truth. "I'm still Max Nartker, and I'm here to tell people about Jesus." I like to imagine Jesus as a baseball fan … probably even a fan of my team, The Detroit Tigers. But wasn't it Jesus who said, "Do you not know that I am to be about my Father's business?" So, Jesus would applaud Max's decision to reflect, revise, and remove obstacles. Jesus would be grateful that Max decided to go forth and "broadcast" to a larger audience.

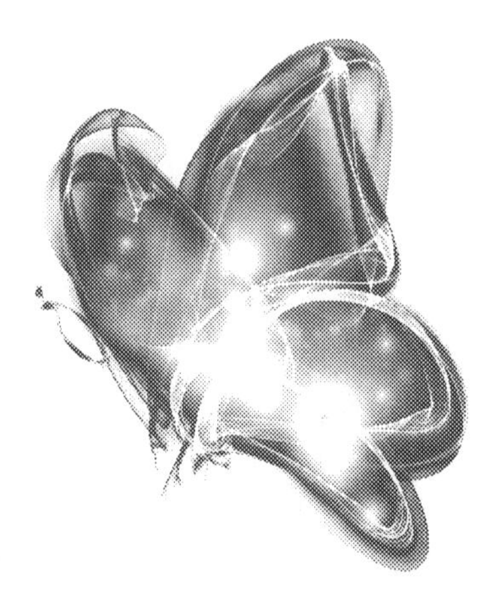

**No life, no matter how short,**
**is insignificant.**

# CHAPTER 21

# Saint Stephanie

*I want to be in that number when the saints go marching in.*

**— Christian hymn**

Churches of the East and the West have their gurus, mystics, seers, holy people, and saints. What really makes a person a saint? A saint is someone who is dead and who, while alive, performed good deeds, even miracles, and is certainly now in Heaven. The Christian Church says, "A person of great holiness, virtue, or benevolence."

That's enough evidence for me. I believe that Stephanie Marie Nartker is a saint!

Some people—maybe you—might disagree. I believe: "Of course she is." Some might say she didn't live long enough. I believe: "No life, no matter how short, is insignificant."

Official canonizers would question: "Who was she? What was she here for? Did she create miracles?"

Stephanie Marie Nartker was the infant daughter born to Linda and Ron Nartker of Midland, Michigan. During her life of only 23 days, Stephanie Marie instilled in Linda and Ron the insatiable desire to add more children to their family through adoption. Stephanie Marie inspired Linda and Ron to travel to Russia and adopt two children, thus removing

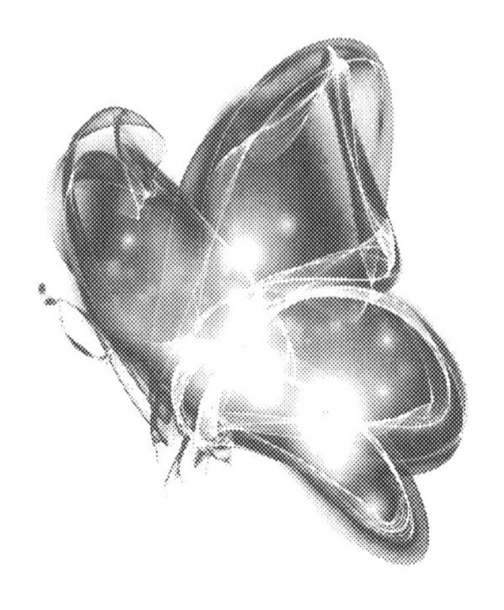

**Can you see the good—the saintliness—in everyone, including yourself?**

them from a crowded orphanage and giving them a life in which they have a greater opportunity to be virtue and benevolence to a greater number of people.

Stephanie lives on within Max and Elena. If not for Stephanie, Max and Elena would not have this American life. Or they would be in Russia, sweeping streets with homemade brooms and hanging laundry in an urban alley. Is that not miracle enough?

Stephanie Marie, during her short life, shifted the lives of others in miraculous ways. She lives on in Linda and Ron. She lives on in Courtney and Eric. She lives on in me and in you.

Is that not miraculous enough? I think so, Saint Stephanie. I think so.

**TIME OUT**

Do you consider Stephanie to be a saint? Think of other people in your life—saintly in their actions or not. Can you consider them to be a saint? Recall that the word *legend* means "the life of a saint." How many of these people are legendary to you? If not, consider who that person is or those people are. Consider what they are here for on this Earth, in this lifetime, as a presence in your life. Do you see their worth and their value even if you don't like their actions? Do you see their benevolence? Can you now consider them to be a saint? Or at least have some few saintly qualities? It might be a stretch, but can you see the good—the saintliness—in everyone, including yourself? Can you see their MaxAbility?

# THE POWER OF *YOU!*

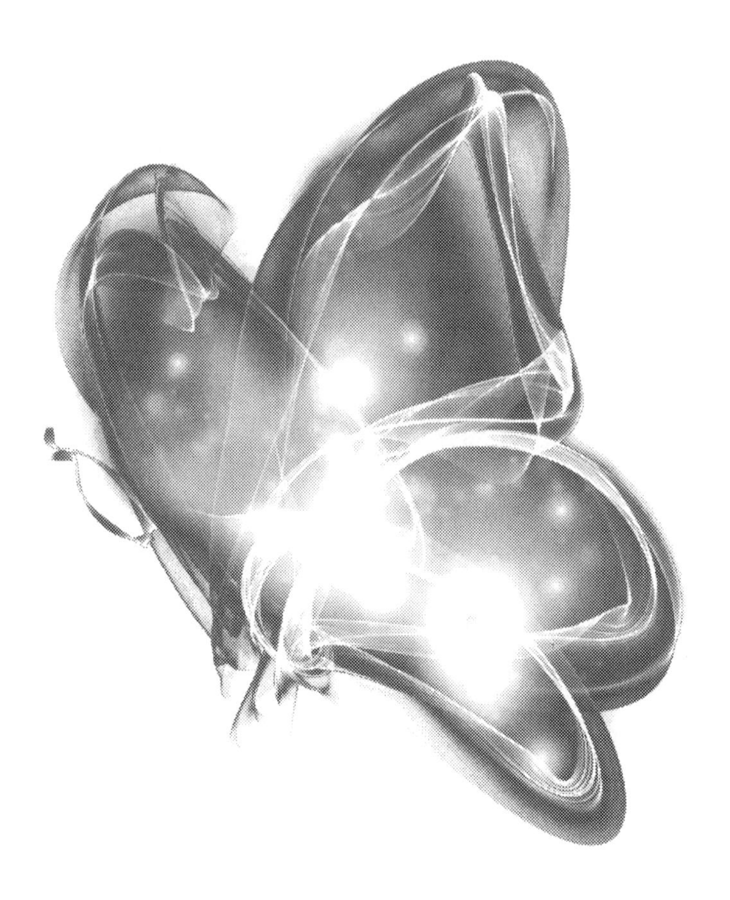

# THE POWER OF *YOU!*

You. Yes, you. Who are you? What forces shape or have shaped you?

In my Catholic/Episcopalian/Christian childhood, I learned the power of me within a community of believers. I learned the power of ritual, of prayer, of faith. I gained knowledge of something greater than myself. I learned about forgiveness, connection, commitment, about the holy and sacred stories that connect us.

Through the years, I have also learned that there are so many other stories that connect us back to the root of our humanity. These stories are not dualistic, opposing, or binary; right or wrong, good or bad, east or west. They simply *are.*

These stories identify us as *one* people sharing *one* universal life. Through *Sportuality,* I attempted to help readers understand win-win, both-and, and a greater level of joy by engaging "the other" on a stage that includes the world of sport as well as the world outside of sport.

This book, *MaxAbility*, is now asking you to do the deep dive into who you are … *really.* And what you're doing here … *really.* Only by asking will the answers come to you. So ask, seek, knock that the door to a life of peace, love, and joy may be always open for you. Yes, you!

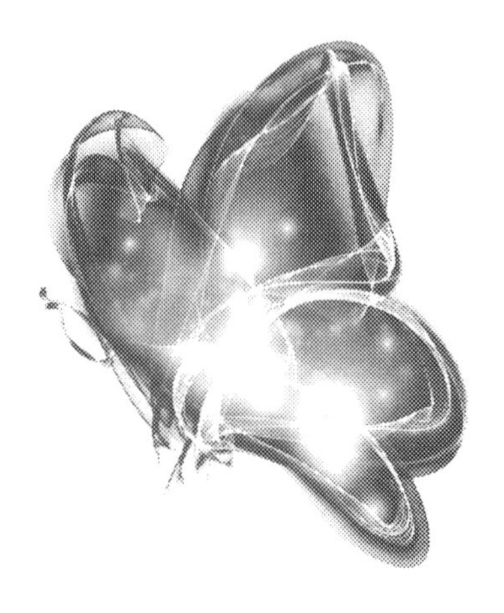

***I am who I AM . . . just as you are.***

## CHAPTER 22

# Overtime Reflections

*"God always offers us a second chance in life."*

**— Paulo Coelho**

I often ask myself: "What if Max and I shared our original conversation again now?"

With that, I am giving myself an opportunity for a do-over—or, as we say in volleyball, a replay. I am giving myself another chance to respond—after having employed what has now been several years of critical thought and analysis of his questions.

Today, I would look Max in the eye, and I would say: "Thank you, Max, for those questions! I am who I AM. I am a blessed child of Creation and a member of the Cosmic Universe, just as you are. I am—and you are—peace and love and joy. I am here to connect and to remind humanity that all thought is connected, all minds are joined as One. Everything we are, everything we do, and everything we create flows into and throughout all human consciousness. And that realm of co-creation is where we find our joy!"

Then I would say to him: "Thank you for crossing my path and journeying with me."

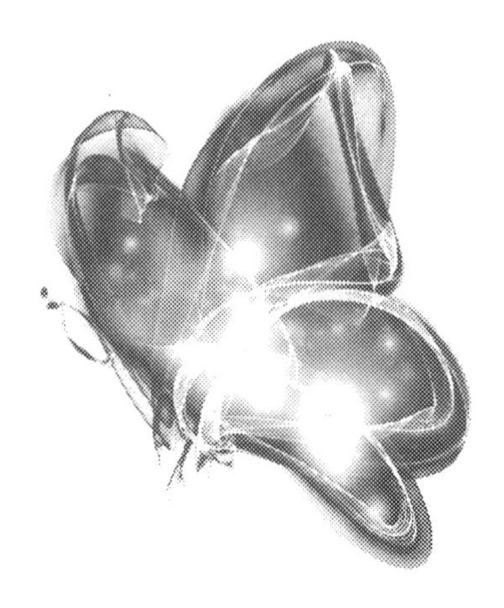

***We are* part of the Divine energy.**
***We are here* to expand the**
**human consciousness.**

So, with that notion that I didn't know then but know now, we come to the end. We come to the place where this entire message is supposed to make sense … to both you and to me. We come to the point where it's all tied up with a neat bow so that you can put this book down and give it to a friend or put it in your neighborhood Little Free Lending Library.

The end of crafting this book also coincides with the impending end of my 35-year coaching and teaching career at Kalamazoo College, which, in this world, encourages those questions to take on a new energy with ever-expanding opportunities.

During those years, my identity was linked to a place: a shared gymnasium and my large private office with an expansive window on the first floor of the Anderson Athletic Center. I attained an identity: coach, professor, advisor, colleague, and associate chaplain. I performed certain actions that allowed my team to experience the world of sport beyond our campus and our league by taking them on international competitive journeys to China, Costa Rica, Trinidad, and South Africa.

Consequently, at this point in my life when I let go of one place, one identity, and one set of actions for others in the great unknown, it has become increasingly difficult for me to write about who *I* am and what *I'm* here for. It's been somewhat anxiety-ridden.

My answers come in waves during meditation, while teaching class, in the heat of competition, while interacting with my family. My answers are changing as I move from career to encore career. This is a bit chaotic. But I find reassurance and peace in a pattern: The answers are more of who I *am* and less about what I *do* … or will do.

I am more and more aware that we—you and I—are part of the Divine Energy. We are here to expand the human consciousness, to add our ideas to the growing number of ideas of others. We—all of us—are here to live our joy and, thus, evolve to expand the world's happiness.

**Let us all now move forward
together in gratitude
and confidence.**

I look upon these answers as my connection with that benevolent force of the cosmos that is filled with ever-increasing miracles. And I find solace in the spirit of Saint Stephanie who reminds me to seek my answers—my own answers—with confidence, void of regret for anything related to who I used to be.

Let us all now move forward together in gratitude and confidence.

# ABOUT THE AUTHOR

Jeanne Hess is currently serving on the Kalamazoo City Commission, having retired as a professor of Physical Education and Volleyball Coach at Kalamazoo College in Kalamazoo, Michigan. She earned her B.S. from the University of Michigan, where she was a member of the Wolverine volleyball team for four years. Volleyball then defined the next 40 years after she met and married Jim Hess, the highly successful girls' basketball and softball coach at Ann Arbor Gabriel Richard High School.

They moved to Kalamazoo as Jim began a coaching job at Western Michigan University, allowing Jeanne the opportunity to earn her M.A. in Exercise Science there; a prelude to her teaching and coaching career at Kalamazoo College. WMU inducted her into the Alumni Honor Academy for Health, Physical Education and Recreation in April 2010.

The 2018 season, her final, marked her 35th volleyball campaign. She sports an overall winning percentage of .508 with 563 wins, five MIAA championships, and six NCAA Division III Tournament appearances. She has led her team on four international trips to China, Costa Rica, Trinidad and Tobago, and South Africa.

The Midwest Region Coach of the Year in 1990 and 1991, Hess served as the AVCA Division III representative to the Board of Directors from 2003-2008. She also served on the University of Michigan Letterwinners M Club Board of Directors from 2012-2019.

In addition to coaching volleyball, Hess has been an assistant for the women's basketball (1991-95) and softball (1996-2001) programs as well as serving as associate chaplain from 2001-2008. In recognition of her outstanding service, Hess was awarded the College's prestigious Lux Esto Award of Excellence in 2014.

Hess and her husband, Jim, reside in Kalamazoo. They have two sons, Andrew and Kevan. Andrew played baseball at the University of Michigan and was drafted by the Detroit Tigers in 2007. Kevan played baseball at Western Michigan University and was drafted by the Detroit Tigers in 2009. Both are now happily married and fathers of 2 children each.

Jeanne published her first book in January of 2012. *Sportuality: Finding Joy in the Games* is a look into the heart of sport and how shifting a thought about sport can be used as a vehicle for higher consciousness and an outcome of joy, love, and peace for all involved.

Printed in the United States
by Baker & Taylor Publisher Services